Overcoming
DEPRESSION

Examines the nature and symptoms of this common illness and gives sound advice on conquering it, including a unique self-help programme.

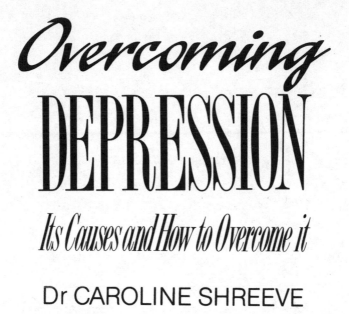

Overcoming
DEPRESSION

Its Causes and How to Overcome it

Dr CAROLINE SHREEVE

THORSONS PUBLISHING GROUP

First published 1984

British Library Cataloguing in Publication Data

Shreeve, Caroline
Depression
1. Depression, Mental—Treatment
2. Self-care, Health
I. Title
616.85'2706   RC537

ISBN 0-7225-1548-0

*Published by Thorsons Publishers Limited, Wellingborough,
Northamptonshire, NN8 2RQ England*

Printed in Great Britain

DEDICATION

This book is dedicated to my husband, David, with all my love, to thank him for his hard work in curing my depression — an essential preliminary to my helping other sufferers do the same.

CONTENTS

INTRODUCTION

At first glance, a book such as this would appear to run the risk of causing one of two responses in the many readers for whom it is intended. It might seem likely to evoke amazement and disbelief, at the sheer presumption of an author who is neither a learned professor of psychiatry nor an academically renowned student of human psychology with numerous clinical trials and research papers to her name.

Alternatively, a book which claims to reveal the secret of how one of man's most distressing illnesses may be overcome, might be considered to be raising false hope among the thousands of depressed patients and their relatives who have hoped so long for a 'miracle cure'.

Because of this, I should like to clear up any misunderstanding from the outset, by explaining that I have not spent years secretly perfecting my own psychoanalytic technique, nor thousands of pounds in privately researching the properties of rare herbs. What I *have* done, is to talk to and observe countless hundreds of depressed people since I first began to practise medicine, in order to discover the factors they have in common and thus work out a reliable method of helping them.

This immediately begs the questions — why a special interest in depressive illness? And, if so, then why not specialize in psychological medicine, treating dozens of depressed people every day, in a psychiatric hospital where there are facilities for their special care and attention?

To answer the first question, I am particularly interested in depression because patients suffering from this illness present a unique challenge which, so far, medicine has failed to meet. Treating depressive illness is completely different from treating, say, an inflamed appendix or a chest infection — and neither surgery nor drugs are capable of curing it. And the thousands of depressed people who attend regular hospital consultations or receive repeat prescriptions for antidepressants — yet remain as depressed as ever — bear witness to the truth of this.

I have, moreover, suffered from the illness myself, and know exactly how it feels to experience what Bertrand Russell called: '. . . that terrible loneliness in which one shivering consciousness looks over the rim of the world into the cold unfathomable lifeless abyss.' And I know the perils that beset the nightmare journey back to normal health — provided, of course, that the sick person can be persuaded to turn away from the mesmerising horror plainly visible to all those who venture, or are driven, to the 'rim of the world' in the first place.

In answer to the second question, I have to ask, 'What facilities?' Most people would agree that the problem of depressive illness will never be solved by prescribing drugs and, apart from critically ill depressed people who require short spells of care away from their home environment, lengthy stays in mental hospitals tend only to worsen the condition.

To sum up my attitude to depression and its treatment, I do not feel that orthodox medicine has the required approach to mentally sick people in general, nor to depressive illness in particular. Certainly, drug therapy and psychoanalysis have useful roles to play in particular circumstances, but these roles are, by their very nature, both specific and limited, and to try to treat all depressed people with antidepressant drugs and a ten minute chat, is as useless as trying to 'cure' an asthmatic with a shot of adrenaline in the arm and a bottle of cough mixture. Certainly a patient in the throes of an asthma attack may obtain temporary relief from these measures. But if you ignore other essential factors, in particular determining the root cause of his asthma and trying to eradicate it, then he will continue to have asthma attacks until the day he dies.

No-one would pretend, continuing to use an asthma sufferer as an example, that it would be possible to rid him totally of his *tendency* to asthma attacks. People are, and always will be, born with certain weaknesses and predispositions, due to the pecularities of their constitution or the genetic pattern they inherit from their parents. A man or woman with an asthmatic make-up will always possess this; but determine, through thorough investigation, that he is allergic to fish or feathers, say, and desensitize him — and much, if not all, of his trouble will be solved.

In the same way, antidepressants can make a depressed individual feel a lot better temporarily. But, if we forget about other forms of essential therapy and neglect to investigate the reason for his episodes of illness, he will remain on antidepressants for life with very little to show after years of such therapy other than deeply rooted depression and a tender liver due to the drugs.

There are many factors in the causes of most serious diseases, and depression is a prime example of this. For this reason, effective therapy is always multifaceted and, although the same principles of treatment apply to all depressed patients, the actual regimen should be tailored to the individual's special needs. I have devised a method of coping with the illness which can be applied to anyone suffering from it provided, of course, care is taken at the outset to obtain a clear picture of a particular patient's symptoms and the manner in which this highly ubiquitous illness manifests in him.

There is nothing especially startling in what I am going to say. A lot of it has been said before, although not all the techniques have been tested and tried out on patients quite as extensively as they warrant. What is new, is the attempt to portray an accurate picture of depression with which depressed people can identify and which their confused friends and relatives can accept and understand. For 'depression' is a frequently-abused term with a precise clinical meaning and, until we establish exactly what we are discussing, no-one is likely to benefit from the advice that follows.

Finally, my approaches to treatment have the advantage that they can be put into effect at home, either by the patient himself as a preventive measure or by his family or friends if he is too ill to cope. I will also show you how to work out the particular regimen most suitable to you, and how to obtain every ounce of benefit from it.

1.

THE NATURE OF DEPRESSION

It is sad — but true — that those very people most in need of a particular piece of advice or information, are frequently the last to receive it. It is especially likely to be true with respect to the information and advice contained in this book for, due to the peculiar nature of the illness with which it deals, deeply depressed people are the least likely to pick up a book and read about how their illness may be overcome.

The reverse is true of most other illnesses. There are often stories in the national press of people with the most daunting handicaps, both social and physical, who learn to cope despite their disadvantages. They marry, often have children, and pursue a full time career despite blindness, disfigurement, loss of a limb, or even a hopelessly incurable disease. They frequently help others with similar problems to cope, too.

The victims of the most serious illnesses are also among the first people to buy new books on their complaint, the moment they appear in the bookshops. Generally well versed in the most recent research and the development of new drugs, many chronic sufferers are anxious to learn as much they can about their condition, and often start their own campaign groups for the pooling and the dissemination of all relevant information.

Not so depressed people — at least, certainly not while they are suffering from an acute attack of their illness. A depressed person *cannot* — by the very nature of his sickness — make any substantial effort to help himself. This is one of the basic facts about the complaint that the sufferer's relatives, friends, colleagues and even doctors fail time and again to realize. For, while an element of the 'fighting spirit' continues gamely to flourish in severely physically handicapped people, the depressed person typically lacks motivation.

To return to my first point — no severely depressed person is in the least likely to read this book. You are most likely, as its reader, to have a general interest in psychology and mental sickness; to be the concerned friend or relative of a depressed person; or to suffer from depression yourself, being at the moment between severe bouts of the illness.

If you fit into the latter category, and are either recovering from weeks of indescribable misery or — even worse — feel as though you are about to enter another such period, then take heart. You *can* put depression behind you for the rest of your life and this book will show you how to do so. In fact, if you can just make the effort to bear this promise in mind, while no doubt remaining sceptical about its validity — you will be doing yourself a very good turn.

You should also remember that a sense of deep isolation is an almost invariable feature of depressive illness. Difficulty in communicating with other people, and in taking in information from them, makes you feel as though an invisible but impenetrable barrier separates you from other people with whom you come into contact. And this sense of 'separateness' is greatly increased by the absence of any obvious signs by which your illness can be identified. In the words of one depressed patient: 'It's just as though all we depressed people have, for some reason, been given the mark of Cain. We are "set apart" from the rest of the human race, at least during bouts of severe depression.'

'The only problem is that no-one apart from us can actually *see* what makes us different.'

Now it is true that depressed people lack an obvious handicap, such as a missing limb, a paralysed arm, or loss of sight. Some chronically depressed people are able, between incapacitating attacks of their illness, to put on such a convincing front that no-one who did not know them intimately would ever guess that they were mentally ill. For this reason, it often comes as a shock to colleagues and acquaintances, suddenly to hear that 'old so-and-so' has just taken an overdose, or been admitted to hospital with a nervous breakdown.

Certainly, a case of severe depression is difficult to miss, and I shall be going into detail about this condition in the next chapter. Suffice to say here, that mild to moderately depressed people may feel quite desparate at their inability to explain what is wrong with them, and resent deeply the fact that they do not look a fraction as ill as they feel. Some depressed people even refuse to go to see their doctor because they have no symptoms or signs to show him and feel quite unable to put their state of mind into words. More is known about the manifestations of depression now, though, than was the case even ten years ago. Now, the experienced doctor should be able to spot certain pointers in a patient's appearance and the way he thinks and talks — even in the apparently unrelated illnesses for which he is seeking advice — to suggest that the underlying cause is depressive illness.

It is deeply regrettable that the complaints of a depressed patient are often dismissed as trivia without the trouble being taken to determine whether a more serious illness lies hidden underneath. Telling a person not to fuss, because he is sleepless, unable to eat and irritable, without first checking whether these complaints are part of the symptomatology of depression, is heartless, ignorant and thoroughly unprofessional.

Doctors *are* only human, however, and as capable as the rest of humanity of failing to observe and interpret what ought to be obvious to them. And when you take into consideration the stress and strain of life today — especially for a busy GP — allowances should be made. After all, with the suicide rate as high as it is nowadays among GPs, the chances are that he or she is trying to battle with depressive illness too.

So do not be deterred from paying your GP a visit, either because you fear that your ability to relate your problems is inadequate, or because he once gave you the brush-off when you consulted him about a minor ailment and you are afraid that he would not understand.

You might be surprised that I am advocating visits to your doctor, when I have already stated that I do not feel that orthodox medicine has the right approach to mental illness, or that it is able to do very much to help patients with clinical depression. As I pointed out, psychotherapy and drug therapy have a definite, if very circumscribed, role to play in the treatment of this complaint, and there are certain circumstances, which I shall discuss in this book, in which orthodox medicine can help alleviate severe symptoms. There is also, on some occasions, a great need for personal contact and the opportunity to talk to someone about depressive signs and symptoms. And I heartily subscribe to the beneficial effect that one-to-one counselling can have.

Besides having a highly isolating effect on the sufferer, depression is renowned as the one serious illness likely to produce reactions of irritation and criticism in family members and colleagues rather than understanding, help and sympathy. People simply cannot readily accept the fact that, since you do not have anything obviously the matter with you, nevertheless you are incapable of 'pulling yourself together' as they generally suggest.

You may feel on these occasions, when endeavouring to cope with life despite symptoms of severe depressive illness, that this kind of attitude in others is having no ill effect on you, simply because you have pretty well reached rock bottom anyway and are long past caring how people react. This may be partly true, in a superficial sense; but the long-term effect of total misunderstanding about your illness serves only to alienate you further from the rest of the world and increase your feelings of isolation and hopelessness.

All diseases are cruel in their own way, but sometimes depression seems to be to be one of the cruellest. No normal person would dream of telling a blind person that they should walk faster, cease to drop objects and dispense with their guide dog or braille books. It is just as inhuman to row with or criticize a depressive for his lack of interest in his surroundings, his tardy mental functioning and his occasional outbursts of irritation.

It is not an overstatement to say that depression is a silent

killer. Most people realize that there is always some degree of
risk that a person suffering from depression may try to commit
suicide. But I have more than the potential suicide risk in mind
when I refer to the destructive powers of this disease. I am
talking about the fact that it slowly and inexorably strangles
joy, desire, hope, peace of mind, and the ability to derive
satisfaction from work, relationships and one's chosen
environment. In fact it goes even further. It removes the *wish*
to enjoy the ordinary pleasures of life, and the memory of once
having enjoyed them. So overwhelming is a depressed person's
feelings of despair, that he cannot be persuaded to make the
slightest attempt to gain satisfaction from anything around him.
This is simply because all the possible courses of action open
to him, appear as useless and pointless as one another.

Besides the intense mental suffering involved in an immediate
sense, this state of affairs also has the effect of causing serious
and often irreversible pathological changes in the psyche and
in the personality. That, quite apart from any other
consideration, is why it is vital for depressive illness to be
recognized and treated at the earliest possible opportunity.

I will give a few instances of patients I have treated, whose
case histories illustrate some of the points I have been
discussing.

During the psychiatric residency weeks of my training as a
doctor, I chose to stay in a very old, very large mental hospital
in Hampshire. It was there that I came across diagnosed
depressive illness for the first time, and during my month's stay
saw the illness in many different stages and degrees. For the
provision of a graphic account of how it actually feels to be
depressed, Malcolm Renny comes immediately to mind. We
saw Malcolm in Out Patients, and he was able to tell us vividly
about what he had just been through, since he had at the time
almost completely recovered from an attack. By contrast one's
powers of description and communication are severely limited
during the course of a severe spell of depression.

Malcolm Renny was a twenty-five-year-old accounts director
with a good degree and four years' experience in advertising
behind him. Successful and highly paid, he had recently
become engaged to the girl he had lived with for a year *and*

been promoted to the particular post he had sought for a long time. Everything in life seemed to be going his way, and he was quite unable to account for the episodes of depression that had caused him to seek psychiatric help. Malcolm told us:

> I have been affected this way since I was in my teens. I have coped more or less until just recently, chiefly by arranging to take leave due to me whenever I sensed an attack coming on — and, until last year, I was getting depressed about twice yearly.
>
> Since Christmas, though (it was then August), I have felt slightly depressed most of the time, and have had three really bad spells. I shan't keep my job much longer if this state of affairs continues, which is why I have been obliged to get some help.
>
> If you want to know what depression feels like, I can only say that it feels like dying. Or at least that is how it seems when you are in the depths of an attack. As I say, I am never really free from depression nowadays, so am constantly having to battle with a lack of energy and enthusiasm, awful periods of self-doubt, and bouts of irritability which are quite foreign to my usual make-up. Sex has been bad too, for about the last six months. I never really seem to feel like making love, and once or twice have failed to get an erection. This scared me terribly.
>
> When I am acutely depressed I am practically prostrate with the illness. The last attack came on all of a sudden and took me unawares — I was alone over the weekend in my flat as Annabelle was abroad on a modelling job. I felt wretchedly miserable on the Saturday and failed to keep a longstanding dinner appointment to which I had earlier been looking forward.
>
> Not only did I not go — I did not even telephone to cancel. I stayed in bed, with the telephone off the hook and the doors bolted, and lay in bed all day Sunday. I was completely incapable of contacting anyone or communicating in any way; I was still in bed when Annabelle returned from Germany on Monday afternoon.
>
> It was all extremely embarrassing, so far as my job was concerned — my boss and my secretary had been trying to 'phone me all morning and, to make matters worse, the dinner engagement I had failed to keep was with a senior colleague.
>
> Annabelle had to pretend that I had been involved in a minor car accident and had been in hospital for twenty-four hours with concussion. Even that story produced problems as we had a devil of a job preventing the firm from sending 'Get Well' messages

and even flowers, to a fictitious private clinic Annabelle had magicked up. Even then, despite all the emergency action required by my fiancée to preserve my reputation with my firm, I couldn't summon up any sense of urgency about any of it.

Annabelle called the doctor and he gave me a sedative. The last thing I needed under the circumstances I should have thought, since I could hardly keep awake as it was. Nevertheless, I took the tablets and slept almost continuously for the next three days. After a rather shaky weekend, I was able to return to the office on the Monday, but have found it very difficult to cope since.

Malcolm's account of his depression describes the type that comes in bouts that are severe but self-limiting, and thoroughly incapacitating while in progress. It is the nature of depressive illness to affect every person in a slightly different way, and also for each depressed individual's pattern to change quite considerably if it continues for more than a year, on average. The bouts of depression, for example, may become longer and/or more frequent, or simply more severe. What *is* almost invariable, is the tendency that depressive illness has to grow worse.

A number of unfortunate people are depressed all the time. Depression can start, either gradually or abruptly (for example, following a tragedy such as bereavement) and continue with more or less the same intensity for months or years. This variety tends to be more readily noticed and recognized as a form of mental illness since, unlike the episodic form, there are no bright, cheerful interludes interspersed with bouts of depression. These can have the unfortunate effect of making the latter seem more like fits of moodiness than a condition requiring diagnosis and treatment.

People with continuous depression are likely to suffer permanent or semi-permanent damage to their minds and personalities at an earlier stage than individuals with episodic depression. This is because, in the absence of the correct treatment, the onslaught upon the psyche of unremitting depressive illness is more devastating than that of periodic illness which alternates with spells of relatively good health.

Here is one more case history, this time involving a patient with continous depressive illness. You will notice that I am only giving examples of different forms of depression in this chapter, and am not going into reasons for the illness arising in these patients nor into their treatment. This is because I am not dealing in this book with conventional treatment, and I am using these case histories only as a means of illustrating the different aspects of depressive illness which I am discussing.

Georgina Bunting was thirty-four years old when I saw her at the Hampshire psychiatric hospital during my student residency period, but looked at least ten years older than that. She was an 'in-patient' during our stay there, and had had numerous spells in this capacity in the past, for she had suffered from depression for about fifteen years and had failed to respond to treatment satisfactorily.

She was far less able than Malcolm Renny to give an articulate account of her feelings. Even allowing for the fact that she was less intelligent than Malcolm and was currently taking large doses of antidepressant drugs, it was still possible to recognize definite signs of deterioration in her personality and cognitive powers which, after years of experience, I unhesitatingly attribute to the destructive potential of depressive illness.

This was substantiated from her early records for, at the time of her first admission to the hospital, the doctor had taken careful notes from Georgina's mother who had been deeply shocked at her daughter's sudden attempted suicide. It seemed that Georgina had been a normally happy child and teenager before her initial attack of depression, which had arisen after the sudden death of her father to whom she had always been very close. She had grown steadily more and more depressed as the months passed, giving up first her hobbies, then her friends, and finally her job, and appearing listless and miserable and perpetually tired.

Finally, without even threatening to take her own life, Georgina had taken a bottle of her dead father's heart tablets together with most of a bottle of brandy, and Mrs Bunting had found her deeply unconscious on her bedroom floor the following morning.

When we first saw her in hospital, Georgina was sitting in a chair all by herself gazing into space. The chair was opposite a blank wall, not a window, and the absolute purposelessness of her gaze, combined with her immobility, at first gave the impression that she was in a catatonic trance (a manifestation of certain forms of schizophrenia).

She responded however, albeit very slowly, to the approach of the consultant accompanied by his four students, and answered the questions put to her, if with obvious reluctance. I went back afterwards to talk to her alone and, while she refused to co-operate at first, I did finally get her to say a few words.

Her voice was monotonous and low-pitched, so much so that it was difficult to hear all that she said. She used short sentences or a word or two in response to my questions and did not bother to deflect her gaze from the bare wall. She whispered to me:

> I've a ball of lead inside me, doctor, and I can never get rid of it. It's all the guilt and fear I've known over the years. There is no hope for a person like me. That't why I'm shut up in a place like this.
>
> But I don't really mind. I don't want to go home. I'm useless and I wish I were dead and if I had the energy I'd have another go at putting an end to all this. But I can't even be bothered to do that. I'll live 'til I die, I suppose, just as we all do — but I know I am being punished and I only wish that I could be sure of dying soon.

Despite her appearance, Georgina had clearly once been pretty. She had soft, curly brown hair, large blue eyes and a slim figure. Before her illness started, she had had several boyfriends and had loved parties, dancing and ice-skating. She might have had a wonderful life, a good job, a happy marriage and maybe a family. And here she was, physically perfect and mentally extremely sick.

I realized then that depression is one of the worst imaginable wasters of human life and potential. I determined that I would one day attempt to find a more successful form of treatment than any of those currently in favour, and aim at freeing at least some of the Georginas of this world from their terrible bonds of crushing despair.

In the next chapter we will take a closer look at what

depression actually consists of, at the clinically recognized forms of the illness and at some of the circumstances in which it commonly arises.

2.

THE SYMPTOMS OF DEPRESSION

Depression is often defined as a 'mood' disorder. It is a state of prolonged melancholia, arising either for no apparent reason or as a highly exaggerated reaction to a trigger event. And as well as this state of profound unhappiness, there is an impairment of physical and mental functions such as work capacity, sleep, sexual interest, appetite and even simple thought processes.

When a doctor sees a patient whom he suspects may be depressed — and the diagnosis is not always obvious in the early stages of the disease — he has first to distinguish between a state of clinical anxiety on the one hand, and true depressive illness on the other. The two conditions have a number of features in common, and only careful attention to what the patient has to say, will reveal which illness prevails.

Generally speaking, anxiety is the fearful anticipation of an event which has not yet occurred, whereas depression can be related to something in the patient's past. But anxiety is inseparable from depression, which means that every depressed patient suffers to a greater or lesser extent from concomitant anxiety; likewise, patients suffering from an 'anxiety state' invariably show some sign of depressive illness as well.

It is also essential to establish the actual significance of the various physical and mental troubles affecting the patient. Many of the signs and symptoms forming an integral part of clinical depression can exist in other forms of mental sickness, or result instead from an underlying physical disease. This is why careful diagnosis in the early stages of depression is vital.

Once the diagnosis has been made, the next step is to distinguish between the two main types of depressive illness, reactive and endogenous.

Reactive Depression
This type of depression can be related to events or circumstances in the patient's experience. A typical 'trigger' event of this type is bereavement. Mourning is a good illustration of the fine dividing line between what we would call 'normal' on the one hand, and pathological or abnormal on the other. Anyone deprived of a loved one can be expected to feel deep grief and loss. So mourning is a natural reaction to death, and a healthy reaction to extreme emotional pain.

Reactive depression following bereavement, on the other hand, exceeds 'normal' mourning in degree, or duration, or both. This 'exaggerated misery', as it is sometimes called, is also accompanied by many physical and mental symptoms, and these offer definite guidelines to the diagnosing doctor when he is eventually consulted either by the patient or by concerned relatives. But, because grief and a melancholic state are expected, at least in the first weeks or months following a personal tragedy, reactive depression may gain a considerable hold over the patient's personality before anything is done about it.

There is one symptom which — when present — helps to distinguish reactive depression from other forms of the illness. This is the type of sleep disorder experienced. A person suffering from reactive depression is likely to have difficulty in getting to sleep at night but, once asleep, can generally expect to sleep the night through. Someone suffering from endogenous depression, on the other hand, is liable to fall asleep shortly after getting into bed, and then wake in the early hours, unable to sleep another wink all night.

Endogenous Depression

This type of depressive illness arises in a person for no reason apparent to the sufferer, and cannot be related to any particular 'trigger' event within his or her recent experience or current lifestyle. Many suggested explanations have been put forward to explain how this type of illness comes about. While no one theory is as yet comprehensive, the very fact that depression can be alleviated by both drugs and psychotherapy is suggestive of an underlying disease process, occurring on at least one, or probably several, different levels simultaneously.

We will look at the two most relevant ones — the psychological and the biochemical — in the next two chapters. But it is important not to forget the importance of other contributing factors such as genetic tendency, adverse social circumstances, personality types, stress and 'trigger factor' overloading. We will take a brief look at these towards the end of this chapter. In the meantime, having established that two main types of depression exist, it would be an appropriate moment to take a look at the most important psychological and physical symptoms of the illness as a whole.

Psychological Symptoms

A multiplicity of psychological symptoms can present themselves in depressive illness, and I will deal with the most important of these briefly. The first that comes to mind, is a feeling of *total despair and hopelessness,* and this, once experienced, is quite discernible from the occasional attack of low spirits affecting everybody at some time or another. A spell of unhappiness caused by a row at work, for example, or the loss of a precious possession, is unpleasant enough while it lasts, but can soon be seen in perspective by a normal individual. The intense misery of depressive illness is overwhelming, and the individual derives no real consolation or comfort from sympathetic friends, or from the realization that all periods of bad luck come to an end. For depression deprives the victim of both belief and hope.

Apathy and inertia are also prominent features. Associated with feelings of hopelessness and despair, is a complete lack of interest in the environment, close relationships with friends and family, love-making, personal welfare and personal appearance. Hobbies, pets, possessions, intellectual pursuits that normally give considerable pleasure to the individual are meaningless in the face of depression, and the feelings of apathy can be sufficiently strong for total oblivion to be sought.

Convictions of self-guilt and unworthiness are serious symptoms. Very many depressed people contemplate suicide solely on the grounds of self-hatred, blame and guilt. These feelings, which are among the hallmarks of depression, do not arise as a result of any blameworthy action of the individual concerned, nor from his or her innate unworthiness, guilt or lack of estimable qualities. They are engendered by a very poor self-image, and from an intrinsic inability to recognize elements, either in the surrounding environment or within the personality, capable of giving rise to optimism or hope.

We will look more closely at the neurotic element of depression in the next chapter, but I will point out here that uncomplicated depressive illness *is* classed from the medical point of view as a neurosis and not as a psychosis. The important difference is that people affected by a neurosis, however seriously ill they may become, do not lose contact with reality — they do not suffer from illusions, delusions or hallucinations. People affected by a psychosis, on the other hand, do lose contact with the real world, and frequently suffer from one or all of these factors.

The difference between a neurosis and a psychosis is important to us in this book, because there is a variety of severe depression which is grouped with the psychotic illnesses — manic-depressive psychosis — and the care and treatment required by such patients differs in some ways from that needed by neurotically depressed people. It is worth remembering that while the feelings of profound unworthiness experienced by the sufferer of straightforward endogenous or reactive depression may seem very far-fetched to the normal friend, relative or counsellor, they do not stem from deluded beliefs in the proper sense of the term.

Someone in the depressive phase of manic-depressive psychosis, however, may well be deluded into believing that he is not merely guilty or unworthy of respect or love, but actually the reincarnation of Hitler, for example, or the perpetrator of mass killings or genocide. Needless to say, the suicide rate in deeply depressed psychotic patients is high unless consummate care is taken with both diagnosis and treatment.

Physical Symptoms

The common factor among the physical symptoms of depressive illness is the 'dampening' effect upon normal function. The appetite decreases and there is a tendency to lose weight, except in patients whose depression is accompanied by a high degree of anxiety with the effect upon that particular individual of compulsive eating or constant nibbling. Thought processes are very slow, compared to the individual's normal rate, and sluggishness is the key word in relation to many bodily functions.

Constipation is common, and the digestive apparatus is frequently affected adversely. Someone in whom anxiety is prominent is inclined to secrete excessive gastric acid, and consequently to suffer from peptic ulceration, heartburn, nausea, vomiting, and the reflux of acid and digestive juices into the foodpipe and throat. The depressed man or woman with a fairly low anxiety level is more inclined to suffer from flatulence, a premature feeling of gastric fullness, bad breath and lower bowel problems.

Headaches are a frequent symptom. These can be related to tense neck muscles, lack or excessive amounts of sleep, drug therapy or stress, but sometimes plague a depressed person for no identifiable reason. Physical clumsiness and inertia are also common, and disincline the patient even more from activity of any kind. Tearfulness is often a major problem, although irritability may well be more apparent at times.

The symptoms discussed above pertain both to reactive and endogenous depression. The most important difference between the two is that extra tactics are required in the case of the former to solve the problem that is acting as the 'trigger factor'. This can involve either taking steps to eliminate the cause of the depression (for instance, an unsuitable job, a marriage that has irretrievably broken down), or accepting a compromise so that the trigger factor loses its power to cause reactive depression. Examples of this might be accepting help in coming to terms with an intolerably painful bereavement, or acceptance of circumstances which have hitherto exerted a depressing effect, such as the failure of a child to go to University or to marry someone 'suitable'.

It is easier to see depressive illness in perspective if you realize that there is a very wide spectrum of human reaction to any given set of circumstances. One person may have a breakdown consequent upon bereavement or divorce, another will find unexpected (or even expected) strength, and cope calmly and efficiently with the crisis and its emotional effects. This is not to say that she will maintain a 'stiff upper lip'; merely that she would go into a grief phase and — quite naturally — suffer, but emerge from it after an average time interval as stable and maybe stronger than before. Another person, by contrast, may never have suffered a personal tragedy in his life; but may be severely affected by depressive illness arising for no identifiable reason.

Always remember that depressive illness is a definable illness, just as measles and glandular fever are. You are not 'peculiar' if you suffer from it, and you should not feel embarrassed about the fact. It is a medically recognized state, arising for a number of reasons in large numbers of people, and possesses universally accepted symptoms and signs. It is — or can be — very responsive to treatment, provided this is carried out correctly and for long enough for the patient to benefit from it. Before we look at the available therapy, though, it is a good idea to identify some of the factors thought to be responsible for depressive illness and decide whether any of them might be the target area of preventive measures.

Genetic Tendency
There is thought to be an inherited tendency towards the neurotic types of depression, and it is certain that there is a substantial genetic element underlying manic-depressive psychosis. A progressive tendency to suffer from the disease exists among individuals closely related to diagnosed cases of the illness, and the likelihood rises to above fifty per cent in identical twins. It is believed that 'genetic vulnerability' may be an essential predisposing factor, but that it is insufficient in itself to cause the disorder.

A large number of environmental disturbances can precipitate this illness. Manic-depressive psychosis has a typically episodic nature, and periods of illness are interspersed with apparently normal interludes. These attacks are commoner in the Spring and Autumn and, while many attacks occur spontaneously, many others are precipitated by a personal loss or emotional trauma. Some people experience both types of attack, and a thirty-year-old woman patient of mine will serve as an example.

Ann Elliott was a highly qualified research worker who had held several important University posts before her final breakdown. She had suffered from endogenous depression as a teenager, and had been put on antidepressant tablets and given a short course of ECT (electroconvulsive therapy), which had helped for a while. Her first spell of serious illness came a year after she had qualified. Following the shock of her mother's sudden death she became acutely depressed and was given sick leave from work, during which time she appeared slowly to recover — only to become manic very shortly afterwards and require immediate hospitalization.

A person in his or her 'manic' phase is as sick as a deeply depressed individual, but in many respects the two conditions are exact opposites. Depressed people *feel* very ill, while by contrast manic people often feel absolutely marvellous. Physically and mentally, their normal reactions and thought processes are accelerated as far above normal as they conversely fall below normal during a depression phase. Far from being inert and apathetic, they rush around in circles starting several jobs, none of which ever gets finished, talking excitedly whilst so doing.

Frequently their conversation shows signs of deluded beliefs or illusions that become quickly apparent to the observer, but seem perfectly logical to the unfortunate patient. During her first manic phase, Ann Elliott attempted to buy ten thousand pounds worth of premium bonds — with a dud cheque. She required six months of intensive therapy before she was able to return to her job, which fortunately had been held open for her.

Regrettably, she lost the job eighteen months later when she became ill again with manic depression. This time, no trigger factor was apparent. She appeared to have recovered from the shock of her mother's death, and had just got engaged to a man with whom she was clearly very much in love. Everything seemed to be going well for her, when suddenly she was arrested for flagrant shoplifting — and was found at the police station to be in a highly abnormal mental condition.

Although she again spent several months in hospital and lost her job, her fiancé stood by her and they married a year later. It was only when they came to me for genetic counselling before starting a family that the familial tendency to manic depression came to light. Ann was an identical twin — and her sister had suffered from the illness for several years. It appeared that their paternal grandfather was affected in this way, too.

Adverse Social Circumstances

There are numerous adverse social circumstances liable to lead to depressive illness. Isolation commonly precipitates severe depression; people frequently affected in this way are the elderly, living either alone or in an Institution to which they do not feel they belong; immigrant women unable to speak the language of their adopted country and unwilling to leave the house in order to meet people; and housewives at home all day looking after small children.

A revealing study of depression in the latter group was carried out by two workers who reported their findings as follows: the illness occurred more frequently in working class women in an urban setting than in middle class women in the same setting, and it was closely related to threatening life events. Whether the women became depressed by these events (such as bereavement, divorce, severe financial problems) depended upon four 'vulnerability factors', namely: the presence in the home of three or more children under fourteen; no outside employment for the woman; the absence of a close and confiding relationship with the husband or a friend; and the loss of the woman's mother before the age of eleven.

Mary Kelly was a patient of mine whose circumstances fitted the above description exactly. She was twenty-three when she first became seriously depressed, and had been married for four years to an Irish publican. During that time she had had first a son and then twin girls, and had been unable to go out to work since halfway through her first pregnancy when her blood-pressure had become seriously raised. Far from having a happy relationship with her husband, she disliked and was frightened of him, since he was frequently drunk and physically violent. She had never known her mother, and had been brought up in a succession of homes, all but one of which she had hated. She needed intensive therapy — and separation from her husband — before her reactive depression showed signs of abating.

Personality Types

There are several personality traits which predispose certain people to depression when they are faced with difficult situations. Highly sensitive, insecure individuals who feel they are under constant disapproving scrutiny by the rest of the world tend to be the subject of severe self-doubt, and become depressed accordingly.

So, too, do immature and emotionally unstable individuals who amplify all kinds of emotional reactions and are renowned for their habit of self-dramatization. When faced with a difficult situation where due consideration is not being paid to their own feelings, such people become distressed, dissatisfied and depressed. Many people in this category have what is known as an 'hysterical personality', and symptoms of depression have been found in as many as eighty per cent of such people in some studies.

Stress

There is no doubt whatever that stress, which is an inseparable component of modern civilized life, is a major factor in generating depression. There are two main groups of people to be considered here. First, people with a reduced ability to cope with difficulties are prone to depression — examples of this are shown in mentally retarded individuals, and also in people whose intellectual powers are only moderately impaired. This is because repeated failure and uncertainty exert a depressing effect.

Secondly, there are individuals with normal or high levels

of intelligence who are constantly surrounded by stressful situations which imperceptibly impair their reserves of energy, drive and enthusiasm. Fatigue, coupled with the 'Cnut syndrome' of never being able to stem the tide of stressful events, eventually takes its toll, and results in frustration, self-doubt, tension, anxiety and depression.

It is difficult for many people to understand why some men and women cope efficiently all their lives with a multiplicity of stress factors, and yet others — with no obvious predisposing personality trait towards inadequacy — succumb far more readily to cumulative stress. The essential thing to bear in mind is that the causes of depression are 'multifactorial', that is, many contributory factors exist, several of which are doubtless required to be present in any one individual before the illness manifests itself.

A patient of mine named Ben Harding had the kind of depressive illness which illustrates the last point clearly. He was a forty-three-year-old managing director who for years commuted to work through rush-hour London, smoked thirty cigarettes daily, maintained an expense account diet at work and at home, and never took any exercise. He worked excessively long hours, entertained a lot at weekends and did not seem to know the meaning of relaxation.

He started to show signs of strain when his workload increased as a result of a number of redundancies within the company; and he became suddenly, profoundly depressed when his eldest son was killed in a motorcycle accident. It turned out, during our lengthy discussions, that his father had committed suicide when he, Ben, was eighteen, after a lifetime of depressive illness, and that his paternal grandmother had suffered from the condition for years. Besides a fairly certain genetic predisposition, there were very likely additional contributory factors of which neither he nor I were aware.

Trigger Factor Overloading
This element among the causes of depression merges to a limited extent with the previous section, but I differentiate between them in that by 'stress' I mean continual bombardment with commonly encountered daily irritants such as driving in

heavy traffic, and being unable to park; looking after several small, fractious children simultaneously in a confined space; or being given a workload — and a deadline — which far exceed one's ability to cope.

By 'trigger factor overloading' I am referring to the simultaneous occurrence of several personal catastrophes or tragedies, such as bereavement, redundancy, divorce and ill-health. A well-balanced person may possess barely any degree of predisposition towards depressive illness, but an overloading of precipitating factors can cause the most stable of people to descend into deep depression.

This occurred to one of my patients, whom no-one would ever have suspected could possibly become depressed. The least neurotic of people, John Pocock was a happy, relaxed, contented man of thirty-eight when he first joined our patient list, with a nice wife and two well-behaved children and a house left him by his grandmother, hence no mortgage. He worked as a self-employed carpenter, and always had plenty of work on hand, since his standard of work was excellent and his prices reasonable.

Then Mary, his wife, became ill and was diagnosed as having multiple sclerosis. He gradually took on less work and spent more time looking after her as she became increasingly disabled. His mother, of whom he was extremely fond, died suddenly of a heart attack. Then his house was burgled, two days after his house contents insurance policy had fallen overdue. A week later he was involved in a car accident, in which he broke his right arm which prevented him from working. Finally, his brother was drowned in a fishing accident and his body was never recovered.

John, understandably, suddenly developed acute depression, and for a time lost completely his ability to 'bounce back' in the face of adversity.

Examples such as this clearly illustrate that every human being has his or her breaking point. The vital thing is to know the warning signs to watch out for, and act before serious depression takes hold. In the next chapter we shall examine the psychological basis for the development of depressive illness.

3.

THE PSYCHOLOGICAL CAUSES

Although it is now accepted that a number of factors are necessary for depressive illness to occur, in-depth investigation into their nature and relative importance is of fairly recent origin. A state of 'melancholia' was recognized by the ancient Greeks, who attributed its occurrence to excessive quantities of 'black bile' in the patient's body; and various remedies throughout the ages have been sought in an attempt to cure the dejection and apathy of people rich enough to afford an apothecary's fee.

But it was not until the present century that medical research was sufficiently advanced to divert some of its attention from the more obvious 'killer' diseases to the, in some ways, more complex problems of mental illness. There is a whole world of difference between present day conditions and the barbaric treatment of the 'mad' in the Middle Ages, with the torture and incarceration the latter had to endure in the name of religion and social good.

Nevertheless, medical science has a long way to go before satisfactory answers are forthcoming to the many questions that still vex workers on the subject of disordered psychology. That we no longer attribute insanity to possession by devils, and whip the victims of delusions and hallucinations in an attempt to exorcize them, is of course partly due to the more enlightened and humane attitude of the medical profession as a whole. But an enormous debt of gratitude is due to the growth of allied disciplines, which have fostered interest, observation and clinical testing into the previously bewildering maze of mental disorders.

The chief of these is, of course, psychology; for, from the firm establishment of the roots of this science in the fertile soil of twentieth century intellect and imagination, have sprung the natural progeny of any great discovery — the suitable means of further investigation (psychoanalysis) and appropriate application (psychotherapy). If it had not been for Sigmund Freud, it is possible that the art and science of psychology would never have developed beyond the most rudimentary stage, and that psychiatry would still be a minor and academically inferior branch of Medicine.

Of the factors known to play significant roles in engendering depressive illness, one of the first to gain universal acceptance was that of psychopathology, that is, the pathology or disordered function of the mind, or psyche. It could hardly have been otherwise because, long before the neuroses and psychoses were identified and described, there was at least general agreement that profound misery, when coupled with inappropriate feelings of guilt and a tendency to self-annihilation, constituted a mental illness.

While little was known about the workings of the mind, either normal or abnormal, before Freud's description of its conscious and subconscious regions, melancholia was recognized as a malady of the spirits and various attempts were made to restore the patient to good health, including the playing of music, the induction of lengthy sleep periods and treatment with herbal remedies.

The problem was that treatment could not progress beyond that of occasional symptomatic relief until more became known about the development and mode of operation of the human psyche. Freud is appropriately named the 'father of modern psychology' for his great work in laying the foundations of psychological science. Needless to say, numerous post-Freudian schools have developed in the meanwhile, some altering a little of Freud's teachings here and there, and others diverging so strongly from his basic tenets as to seem in complete opposition to all he believed and taught. Nevertheless, many of the leading exponents of present day psychological theory, owe on analysis a considerable debt to Freud's premises.

Freudian Theory

Sigmund Freud (1856-1939) described the human mind as consisting of two main regions, comparable to an iceberg. He differentiated between the *conscious region,* which he compared to the visible tip of the iceberg projecting above the surface of the ocean, and the *unconscious region,* represented by the remaining massive region invisible below the surface of the water. To the conscious region, he assigned the thoughts, feelings and wishes of which we are aware from one moment to the next in a waking state. To the unconscious region, he assigned the records we all keep of past experiences, sensations and feelings — in fact, he saw it as a sort of 'memory bank' containing details of every occurrence in our lives up to the present time, including those that occur in the early infancy period.

When he later came to describe the various forms of mental sickness, he traced each back to conflicts arising between the conscious mind and subconscious instincts in the three main periods of psychological development, which he named the oral, anal and genital phases. Depressive illness he saw as originating during the oral phase, that is, between birth and the age of one year. To understand how Freud arrived at this conclusion, it is necessary to review the principle points of his teachings.

Freud published his definitive work, *The Ego And The Id,* in 1922, and his terms *ego, id* and *superego* are still in everyday use. The id is chronologically the first of these personality factors to present itself, and it is the only one operative in a new-born baby whose sole standard for reference is its own needs and wants. The id principle is pure instinct; a baby's feelings and reactions result from the satisfaction or frustration of its instinctive needs for sexual gratification and self-preservation. And if mentioning that an infant has sexual instincts seems absurd to you, it is essential to remember that to Freud, sexuality was an extremely broad term.

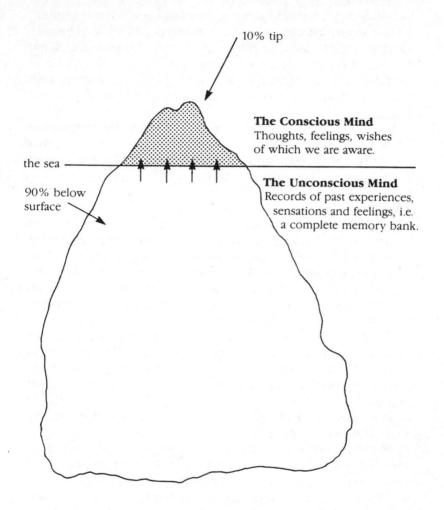

10% tip

The Conscious Mind
Thoughts, feelings, wishes
of which we are aware.

the sea

90% below
surface

The Unconscious Mind
Records of past experiences,
sensations and feelings, i.e.
a complete memory bank.

Figure 1: The Mental Iceberg

He is sometimes accused by his critics of attributing what adults recognize as sexual desire to infants and young children. This is an absurd and unfortunate misrepresentation of Freud's teachings that has done him a great deal of disservice. What he meant by an infant's sexuality was the sexual instinct in embryonic form, latent but vital, waiting to develop along with the other normal instincts and faculties while physical sexual maturity is reached.

Since it is within the oral phase that the conflicts leading to depression arise, we will look in some detail at this developmental phase and allude only briefly, for the sake of forming a complete picture, to the other stages.

The Oral Phase
The newborn baby needs love, security, warmth and nourishment — these are essential to its continuing existence in an environment otherwise alien to it, and it is the instinct of self-preservation that prompts it to demand these elements vociferously when they are not being supplied. At the same time there is present an embryonic sex instinct, or early *libido*, also demanding gratification.

To the small infant, this early sexual need is capable of gratification in a very simple way, for the organ of primary sexual importance at that age is the mouth. Breast-feeding is, therefore, satisfying to the baby in much more than the obviously apparent sense of giving it nourishment. It supplies its need both for sexual gratification on the one hand, and for bodily nourishment on the other.

Two main psychological problems present themselves within the first year of life; the first of these is the conflict that arises between the urge towards self-preservation on the one hand, and the need for sexual gratification on the other, and the two sexes are equally affected but by different means. The boy baby soon realizes that his mother, provider of all his requirements, is also 'of the opposite sex' and she becomes to his infantile mind, a desirable erotic object. At the same time, however, father is revealed to him, both as another person and as *male*, and therefore, being older and stronger, bound to be successful if the two of them rival one another for the mother's love.

He, the baby, can therefore either compete with father and continue to love his mother in a 'sexual' sense, thereby threatening his only source of gratification and nourishment which the angered father may well remove from him; or he can deny his own need for sexual gratification and 'give up' mother as a source of erotic pleasure, causing himself terrible frustration but at least ensuring that his supply of basic necessities continues.

This conflict causes anger at the father, worry at the outcome, frustration at the choice to be made, and guilt at the intensity of his feelings. Much parental love and reassurance are required at this stage for the conflict to be satisfactorily resolved.

The experience of the girl child is similar in that she is faced with a similar apparent choice, the father in her case being revealed as 'male' and therefore desirable, and her mother as the rival and therefore the possible source of trouble. Loving her father may well mean the withdrawal of affection, nourishment, security and oral gratification by her mother; 'shutting off' her sexual feelings for father, while ensuring the continuation of all that she requires physically, is bound to result in extreme frustration of her libido.

If these early conflicts are resolved satisfactorily, then psychological development progresses normally to the next stage. If the conflicts remain unresolved, a tendency arises towards the establishment of an 'all-or-nothing' personality in later years. This is because the infant, in the circumstances just described, seems to be faced with an all-or-nothing choice when seemingly having to choose between father and mother, and this turmoil imprints itself on the child's psyche if the conflict is not properly overcome.

The all-or-nothing personality, seen in adolescence or adulthood, is characteristically one of extreme emotions. Either he (or she) is blissfully happy and content or exceedingly despondent and miserable. This puts one in mind of the illness of manic-depressive psychosis, but in fact the more common outcome of this early formed tendency is that the foundations are laid for later schizoid personality traits to appear. You will notice that I use the word 'tendency' in connection with these early psychological turmoils and their outcome. Unresolved infantile conflicts do not of themselves *cause* an individual to develop schizoid personality traits later in life, or to suffer from depressive illness, or indeed any other neurosis. Their effect is to create a predisposition towards a particular form of mental state which will develop only if the other necessary precipitating factors are present.

The second major problem babies of both sexes have to face, is that of frustration as a result of interference by external factors with their source of gratification. Suppose a small baby is being contentedly breastfed; he or she is gaining oral gratification, nourishment and pleasure, together with bodily warmth, a feeling of security and — if the baby is male — close proximity to the object of his rudimentary erotic feelings, too. A sudden demand for his mother's attention in another direction, either by another child, his father, or any one of a thousand different domestic factors, will cause a sudden cessation of all the infant is enjoying for no reason whatever that is apparent to him.

The effect of this peremptory withdrawal is rage, frustration and self-blame! The tiny child is incapable of working out why his source of pleasure and gratification has been withdrawn and instead of directing his anger at the factor which caused this frustration, he blames himself and resents his own un-worthiness and inadequacy in retaining that which was precious to him.

It is not difficult to see that this psychological process might produce very deleterious effects if a basic habit of 'rage turned inwards' is permitted to establish itself. If, instead of leaving the disturbed infant to scream when breast or bottle-feeding is suddenly interrupted, one or other parent cuddles, comforts and reassures him, the slight tendency to blame frustration on himself will be rendered harmless. But if, instead, the child is shouted at for crying, or allowed to do so for hours without any attention being paid to him, then a conditioned response is set up in his mind which can predispose to depressive illness in later years.

Offering a child solace when he is puzzled, angry and worried, is not the same thing as giving in to his every whim. It is during the first year of life that a small child starts to learn elementary facts about the people in his life and the nature of his environment, and the ego or 'self' factor begins to develop. Its function is to help the infant to cope with the frustrating factors that surround him, in order that his efforts may be appropriately channelled for the achievement of whatever end is in view. As the child grows older and starts to reason, this 'channelling' often takes the form of deliberate naughtiness or playing up in order to get his own way.

Parents have to differentiate between spoiling a child by allowing themselves to be dominated by his wishes; and extending the love, warmth and reassurance he needs — particularly at moments of infantile trauma and crisis.

How does the conditioned response of 'rage turned inwards' result in a tendency to develop clinical depression in adolescence or adulthood? Or in the establishment of schizoid tendencies or even frank schizophrenia? We have noted that the all-or-nothing response sets the scene for later schizoid traits. The inwardly-directed rage has the effect of producing a defence mechanism known as 'dissociation', by means of which the infant dissociates the pleasure he receives from sucking at the breast or teat, from the actual activity involved. By switching off his capacity to experience gratification he protects himself to a certain extent from the pain of future disappointment, but at the same time his subsequent actions become mechanical and provide no pleasure or gratification for him.

By repressing his ability to experience gratification, the infant simultaneously represses his libido and his innate urge to achieve erotic satisfaction. This is a potentially dangerous state of affairs, and can result later on in schizoid personality traits or schizophrenic illness, both of which are characterized by particular types of psychological dissociation.

If dissociation does not take place, the rage-turned-inwards coupled with the self-blame, guilt and self-abnegation sets the scene for future depressive illness.

Another possible outcome of the enormous tension which can be generated at the infant stage of psychological development, is the adoption of compulsive habits in later childhood, adolescence or adulthood.

I said that I would refer very briefly, for the sake of completion, to the other two stages of psychological development. The *anal* stage lasts from the end of the first year of life until about the age of three years. This time is characterized by preoccupation with the problems of gaining bowel control, and establishing a more mature relationship with the mother who — the infant discovers — can be hurt and enraged by his non-compliance with her wishes regarding toilet training. The area of erotic gratification during this period is the anus rather than the mouth, and the small child can gain satisfaction and gratification, if the mood takes him, from withholding faecal material inside his rectum rather than expelling it to please his mother.

Conversely he can dirty himself to enrage or punish her. He can learn, if the circumstances favour his doing so, to gain considerable pleasure merely from inflicting pain on her. Sadomasochistic tendencies originate during this developmental phase, and the reason for its other name of 'anosadistic phase' is easy to see.

Besides sadomasochism, unresolved conflicts arising in this period can result in a predisposition towards hypochondria, paranoid tendencies or obsessional traits.

The *genital* phase starts at around the age of three years, and extends to about six or seven years, to be followed by a latent period which lasts until puberty. It is characterized by considerable curiosity about the genital area, together with anxiety about the phallus or male organ, its presence or absence in the child him- or herself, and the reason for gender differences. Anxiety which is never resolved, or perhaps augmented by refusal of parents to discuss early sexual queries, can transform these early, normal sexual feelings into fear, inhibition and guilt.

Tendencies towards hysterical symptoms, and the anxiety state with its different manifestations including phobia formation, can result from unresolved genital phase problems.

The above account is essentially a simplistic statement of Freud's theories regarding the structure, function and malfunction of the human psyche. His chief contribution to the subject of depressive illness was contained in a paper published in 1917 entitled *Mourning and Melancholia*, in which he pointed out the parallel between the two states (depression was then known as melancholia). He mentioned that both show, 'a profoundly painful dejection, abrogation of interest in the outside world, loss of the capacity to love, [and] inhibition of all activity'. But he also pointed out the characteristic loss of self-esteem in melancholic patients which grieving patients do not show.

In contrast to mourning, which is an energetically charged process consisting of the healthy discharge of the grief with the full co-operation of the person's ego, melancholia (depression) is typified by the low energy content of both body and mind, which undermines the ego and produces the 'depressed', non-alive and unresponsive condition.

This is easier to understand if we remember that the ego or 'self' principle develops during the first year of life, for the express purpose of so directing the infant's activities that they achieve the maximum effect. It governs the id principle, in other words, so that desirable goals are reached which might remain unattainable were the individual to rely solely upon the impulses of his primitive instincts — upon his id.

In mourning, therefore, the ego or directive principle comes to the aid of the afflicted man, woman or child, permitting grief to be discharged effectively and in a manner which contributes to the ultimate recovery of the person concerned. The crying, shouting and screaming which form part of a natural bereavement reaction, enable the feelings or libido invested in the lost love object to be withdrawn so that they may be available for other future relationships. But when a person refuses to deny the reality of the loss he has suffered, he continues to hold on mentally to the lost object, to avoid the pain of separation.

Separation therefore remains incomplete, the ego remains bound up in the lost love object and is depleted and limited as a result.

Freud — as we have seen — postulated that loss of security and love during the oral stage, predisposed in the ways I have described to the formation of a depressive personality, but the absence of any recognized or acknowledged loss in the mind of depressed patients still puzzled him.

Present theory offers the explanation that the loss is not

admitted. The patient modifies his or her behaviour to prevent the acknowledgement of loss, while all the time his ego remains tightly bound to the lost love object and is therefore unable to function properly. The causative loss generally occurs during the oral phase, as Freud suggested, but may be related or at least greatly augmented by the death of a parent during early childhood, or some equally traumatic loss.

Freud summarized the difference between mourning and depressive illness when he said, 'In grief the world becomes poor and empty, in [melancholia] it is the ego itself.' However painful the experience, mourning is, in some ways, easier to live through than severe depression. The majority of bereaved people manage ultimately to come to terms with their loss; and if they experience difficulty in 'letting go' at least the psychotherapist has a relatively easy task to perform in one sense — the loss is identifiable and known to the patient, and analysis does not have to be used to discover the nature of the underlying problem.

The depressed person, on the other hand, often possesses knowledge of traumatic loss at a deep level in his subconscious mind only, and is unaware of its nature. All the same, pain is being suppressed rather than allowed an outlet, and so much psychic energy is involved in this suppression that all the vital aspects of the individual's personality are reduced. Depression is essentially a loss of feeling, desire and excitement, and a characteristic experience of a depressed person is that of 'depersonalization'; more than simple loss of self-esteem, he has suffered the ultimate loss — that of himself.

Karl Abraham was one of the early analysts who, like Freud, attributed adult depression to experiences in early infancy. Abraham made a particular study of manic-depressive patients, and thought that the depressive element was a recurrence of what he named the 'primal depression of infancy'. Babies and young children, according to this theory, underwent many unpleasant experiences during the early years of their lives, as a result of which they developed resentment and hatred towards their parents — particularly towards their mother. For many reasons, this feeling had to be suppressed, and the act of suppression sapped the energy of the patient and weakened him. Depression for Abraham meant not only loss of love but also the suppression of the hatred consequent upon this loss.

It is worth mentioning here that one of the factors operative in suppressing feelings of filial hatred would be Freud's superego. Just as the ego develops after the id, and helps to govern and control it, so the superego develops after the ego, and is represented by what we call 'conscience', or moral sense. It is 'wrong' to hate one's parent, and this social belief becomes inculcated into the child's psyche together with the multiplicity of other ethical and moral tenets which most children come to accept. The weakening of the ego, as Abraham saw it, resulted from the compound effects of anger and hatred; the energetic suppression of those unacceptable emotions; and intense guilt.

The psychologist Melanie Klein was another interesting post-Freudian analyst. She made a special study of the phenomenon of infantile depression, and treated many very young children with this condition. She recognized two major developmental phases through which all children pass, and she referred to them as 'reaction patterns'. The first of these, known as the *paranoid-schizoid position*, refers to the reaction of the infant towards the frustration of his desires and gratification by his mother, which he regards as a type of persecution.

The second stage, which Miss Klein called the *depressive position,* comes into being when the child develops a conscience (that is, when the superego begins to operate) and starts to feel guilty about his negative feelings towards his mother. She wrote:

> The object which is being mourned is the mother's breast and all that the breast and milk have come to stand for in the child's mind: namely, love, goodness and security.
>
> All these are felt by the baby to be lost, and lost as a result of its own uncontrollably greedy and destructive phantasies and impulses against his mother's breasts.

Such an outcome would be particularly likely to occur in a society which discouraged breast-feeding or limited it to two or three months after birth. Under these circumstances one can understand the postulated sequence of frustration-anger-loss, but this would not apply in cultures where to breast-feed for a year or so after birth is normal practice.

We have now looked at the basic principles of Freudian theory regarding human psychology and the manner in which depressive illness comes about. We have also looked briefly at the ideas of two post-Freudian psychologists and noted their similarity to, and also their points of divergence from, Freudian teaching.

In the next chapter we will take a look at the biochemical factors that predispose an individual towards depressive illness.

4.

THE BIOCHEMICAL CAUSES

As we saw from the last chapter, depression has been recognized for many years as a mood disorder. No longer regarded as a bi-product of excessive or imbalanced humours as the Greeks believed, enlightened medical thinking gradually evolved the idea of depression originating as a type of, and also as a result of, disordered mental processes. The work of Freud, and those who followed in his footsteps, allowed this notion to evolve scientifically from the solid foundations of twentieth century psychology. Regardless of the current thinking of the age, however, whether it be possession by devils, humoral imbalance or problems originating deep in the subconscious mind, physical means have always been sought for the relief of depressive illness. Not all the physical beatings, water duckings and brandings with hot irons of the Middle Ages resulted from the sadistic intent of a depressed person's tormentors. Some of these methods represented crude, physical attempts to harry the evil spirit from possession of the individual's mind and soul, freeing the unfortunate victim from demonic possession.

Likewise, the technique of bloodletting and the administration of purges, emetics, carminatives and cathartics were designed to free the patient from melancholic symptoms by one means or another. The idea of bloodletting for melancholia was no doubt a corollary of the idea that excessive quantities of black bile inhabiting the body was responsible for the underlying problem. Bleeding, cupping and leeching were supposed to make the human body an unreceptive abode for demons and evil spirits; and for this reason it is difficult to differentiate between the apparently crude methods of treatment belonging to the Middle Ages proper, and the embryonic beginnings of modern methods. Suffice to say that inducing the removal of any fluid substance from the individual's person, whether it be blood, stomach contents, bowel waste, urine or merely intestinal gas, was a natural development from the old exorcism notion and an essential preliminary step towards treatment with medicinal preparations. Remedies for melancholia have included infusions and concoctions from a wide variety of plants. The range extends from cabbages, Dog's Grass and Feverfew to the Peony, Marshmallow, Tansy and Spleenwort. Magic, of course, was resorted to and the wise man or woman of the community asked to provide a magic potion or charm against melancholia, or perhaps to perform some sympathetic magic to relieve the patient of his symptoms.

All the various forms of antidepressant therapy mentioned so far were aimed at the symptomatic relief of the illness only; for, while the origin of the disease was considered to lie exclusively within the psyche of the patient, various of his symptoms proved to be responsive to some of the medicaments mentioned. It was not until the present century had progressed for several decades that the theory of a specific, or series of specific, biochemical defects as causes of depressive illness was formulated. The history of the birth of this idea is interesting, and worth relating briefly. In 1889 Thiele and Holzinger, two German pharmacologists, synthesized a substance named iminodibenzyl and provided a detailed account of its chemical properties. Its pharmacological attributes were not investigated until 1948 when the German chemist Häfliger produced a series of more than forty derivatives of this compound for possible use as antihistamine drugs, anti-Parkinson treatment, sedatives and analgesics. One of these derivatives, named imipramine, a dibenzazepine compound, was among the few compounds selected for therapeutic trial on the basis of the success achieved with it as a sedative and hypnotic in animals.

Imipramine was allied to the phenothiazine class of drugs and it was discovered by the researcher Kuhn, quite by chance, in 1958; but, unlike the other drugs in this group, imipramine was relatively ineffective in calming agitated psychotic patients. Instead it had a remarkably beneficial effect upon a number of patients suffering from depressive illness.

When Kuhn investigated this drug further he found that, when administered to fifty patients suffering from a variety of depressive syndromes, it produced its most beneficial results in those suffering from endogenous depression.

This group of endogenously depressed patients were characterized by withdrawal into themselves, apathy and inactivity. By contrast, he found that patients who were hyperactive and agitated and depressed were made worse by the drug. Reasons, of course, were sought why imipramine should elevate the mood of depressed people and, little by little, as information from various workers in the field accumulated, the 'Bio-amine theory' of depressive illness was born. This is a very complex field, so I will only present a brief outline of it here. The focal point of the study is brain chemistry and, while a great deal more information is yearly being added to our sum total of knowledge of this fascinating subject, the intricacies of the explanations at a biochemical level are more suited to a textbook dealing with molecular biology than to one discussing depressive illness. So I will keep my outline as simple as possible.

The various functions of the brain, which include the control of our sensory faculties such as sight, hearing and speech; our movements, breathing, heartbeat, balance, and co-ordination; and, in fact, the sum total of all our bodily processes, are known to occur by means of the transmission of electrical messages or impulses from one cell to another. The so-called 'grey matter' of the brain is made up of millions of nerve cells or neurones and the whole brain has been extensively investigated in order to discover which areas of it are responsible for which bodily functions. Control of respiration, heartbeat and endocrine function, for example, has been found to be situated not in the cerebral hemispheres, but at a lower and more primitive area of the brain, the mid-brain and brain stem.

The most sophisticated activities, which tend to differentiate man from other mammals, are controlled by the upper regions of the cerebral hemispheres. Thought processes, emotions, desires and feelings are now known to take place in these complex and convoluted outer layers of the grey matter. These functions originate in their respective areas and take place by means of the passage of the stimulatory impulses along the pathways of the nerves or neurones concerned.

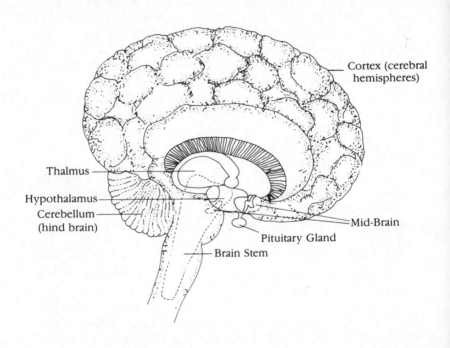

Figure 2: The structures of the brain (a section).

A clear example of a nervous pathway is seen when a thought, arising in our upper cerebral regions, initiates a physical activity. Suppose you are sitting in a chair and the thought comes to you that you wish to stand up, turn round and walk out of the room. This is so usual a thing to do that it does not afford you a moment's conscious consideration, but highly complex electrical activity takes place first in your brain and then in the nerves leading to the muscles of your limbs, before such a wish can be put into operation. The wish impulse, for instance, has to be conveyed to the area known as the motor gyrus. The impulse has then to be transferred along a complex series of pathways to the 'motor' or 'activity' nerves, supplying your arms, legs and the muscles of your back and trunk. Only in this way will your 'sudden decision' to get up and leave the room become actual.

Nervous tissue is so constructed that nervous (electrical) impulses travel within it with ease and great rapidity, but the nerve cells themselves are arranged in such a way that gaps, or synapses, occur at intervals along the length of a particular pathway. One neurone comes to an end and another begins, and in order for the electrical message to leap the gap or synapse,

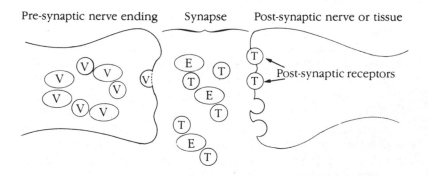

Figure 3: Nerve synapse and neurotransmitter. V = storage vesicles for neurotransmitters; T = neurotransmitter such as serotonin, noradrenaline; E = enzyme such as monoamine oxidase (MAO) which breaks down neurotransmitter.

specific chemical agents, known as neurohumoral transmitters or 'neurotransmitters', are brought into play. This concept of the chemical mediation of nerve impulses is of very great importance to many drugs and of profound importance to our concept of the chemical basis of depression.

Granules of the neurotransmitter chemicals (called 'amines') are made and stored in the terminal part of one neurone and released when an impulse reaches that particular synapse and is ready to be transmitted. The granules of neurotransmitter substance are usually broken down and inactivated, once the transmission across the gap has been completed.

Under normal conditions, then, a nerve impulse in one of the neurones with which we are concerned — say a thought neurone — will travel along the neuronal length, reach the synapse and granules of the relevant chemical will be released into the surrounding fluid. The impulse will, in this way, be 'helped' across the gap, the message will be conveyed and passed on down the following neurone and the granules of the transmitter will cease their activity. The amine neurotransmitters of interest here are either 5-hydroxytryptamine *(serotonin)* or catecholamine (the word 'catecholamine' is an inclusive term covering, amongst other things, *dopamine* and *noradrenaline*).

If we refer to the neurotransmitters involved in emotional activity and the regulation of mood as 'the amines' in this particular instance, you will understand what is meant by the statement that many cases of depression have been found to be due to a disturbance of amine metabolism. Serotonin and noradrenaline are the most important in this context and it is a functional deficiency of these two substances that is thought to constitute the major biochemical defect in depressive illness. Most readers will have heard of noradrenaline. It is closely related to the substance adrenaline, with which nearly everybody is familiar, and as its major role in depressive illness has come to light over the past few years it has been referred to in scientific reports appearing in the national press more and more frequently. Serotonin may also be a familiar name. It is the brain substance with which hallucinogenic compounds, such as LSD, psilocybin mushrooms and similar substances interfere; and its name appeared quite often in the newspapers in the 'sixties, when articles began to be written on hallucinogenic compounds and their effect on brain function.

Serotonin has also been mentioned recently in the press in connection with the amino acid L-tryptophan. This is a naturally occurring antidepressant substance, at present freely available through health food shops. I will be referring to it again in the chapter dealing with the action of antidepressant compounds.

Dopamine is less likely to be a familiar term. One of the catecholamines, it is thought to play a large part in the neuronal transmission of mood and feeling, and to be especially involved in the depression of old age. Depression occurring in the later years of life is thought to be due, in particular, to a deficiency of this substance. The dopamine content of the brain diminishes considerably after the age of forty-five and pronounced fall in dopamine levels is known to account for the development of Parkinson's disease, as well as the high incidence of depressive illness and the decline of male sexual vigour. The reason that a single brain defect can account for the loss of co-ordination in patients with Parkinson's disease, as well as for depression and impotence, is that dopamine plays a major part in the regulation of all three functions.

Hormonal Variations

There is no doubt that a number of hormonal changes are closely related to depressive illness and it is worth considering in particular, as an example of this, the type of depression peculiar to young and middle-aged women.

I am referring to three different varieties of the illness — premenstrual, post-natal and menopausal. In all of these cases, there is, without any doubt, a decisive hormonal factor in the production of the condition as well, very probably, as an innate predisposition to depressive states. All women suffering from hormone-related depression require careful diagnosis and management, and my own feeling is that it is a very good thing if hormone therapy can be avoided.

Premenstrual Depression: A lowering of mood, coupled with irritability, fatigue, inertia and reduced self-confidence are predominant aspects of the premenstrual syndrome (PMS) which affects the majority of women in the week to ten days prior to the onset of their periods. While some women notice minimal change during that time, others are more seriously affected and one woman in four has her life (job, work, home, marriage) seriously disrupted by it. Depression does not always feature in PMS, but when it does so it is frequently severe, and has occasionally been known to result in suicide. Particularly apparent in PMS depression, are feelings of guilt and unworthiness, and these are worsened both by the uncomfortable physical symptoms and the irritability element which frequently prevents women from responding to understanding and sympathy extended by partner and family.

Post-Natal Depression: This is a serious form of depression thought to be brought about by hormone imbalance during the early post-natal period, coupled with an intrinsic predisposition to depression which, before the onset of the illness, is often unsuspected. Other precipitating factors are a stressful domestic situation, excessive tiredness, the emotional impact of giving birth, and a lack of physical fitness.

Psychotic elements sometimes appear in post-natal depression, and the new mother may entertain fantasies — which terrify her — of either murdering her child, or at least severely harming it. Psychological contact with reality is frequently lost, and hospitalization is often essential.

Menopausal Depression: Depression frequently occurs as an aspect of the 'change of life' and may occur alone or as part of a complex picture of menopausal disturbance. The current trend in the management of this condition is to give hormone replacement therapy for a combination of physical and psychological symptoms and an antidepressant for depression alone.

5.

MEDICAL THERAPY

We saw in Chapter Three the means by which unresolved conflicts in infancy and childhood can predispose an individual to depressive illness later in life, and we saw in Chapter Four how the existence of certain biochemical defects can further contribute to an innate tendency towards the illness. It is worth reminding ourselves at this stage that the causes of clinical depression are multifactorial; that is, several different factors must be present for the condition to come about.

I mentioned earlier that depression is a definitive illness with a recognized aetiology (causative factors); presentation (the manner by which it affects people); signs and symptoms; and prognosis. This makes it clearly comparable to, say, glandular fever, a severe head cold or multiple sclerosis. And it is not only depressive illness or, indeed, mental illnesses as a whole that require a number of contributory factors to be present before they arise. A common complaint like influenza, for instance, demands the presence of an infecting virus, its transfer to the nose, throat and mucous membranes of the prospective patient, insufficient antibodies against it to protect the individual and some predisposing factor, or factors, in the physical condition of the patient which allow him to succumb and develop influenza.

If I appear to be labouring this point of depression as a

recognized clinical illness, it is for a very good reason. Once *you*, as a sufferer from depression (or as the relative or friend of a depressed person) can convince yourself that the condition we are discussing is a clinical state, in common with many others, it will appear only logical to you that some form of effective treatment can exist. As I said in the first chapter, one of the greatest difficulties a depressed person faces is that of accepting the fact that they may one day be cured. Certainly it would be very difficult indeed, if not impossible, to convince a person who is in a severe state of depression that he may one day recover, for he lacks sufficient motivation even to 'wish' for this. Depression is a state of varying degrees of mental pain, and severe depression is a state of mental agony pervaded by a sense of astonishment that continued existence from one moment to the next is even possible. It is as impossible to get through to an individual in that condition and persuade him that he should feel hopeful, as it would be to convince a woman in the throes of a painful labour, or a road accident victim who has just broken both legs, that she or he will soon feel better.

Accepting that depression is a medical condition as opposed to a phase in your life, during which you are a changed and helpless person, gives you two real advantages. If you can bring yourself to say to yourself and to other people, 'I sometimes get depression,' or 'I sometimes suffer from depression,' rather than 'I get depressed,' or 'I have a depressive personality,' then you will start to regard your condition objectively, just as you might arthritis, an allergy or asthma. Convincing your conscious and your subconscious mind that depressive illness is no more or less than a syndrome which can be defined, classified and inserted neatly into a textbook category, enables you to take the first very important step on the road to objectivity.

We saw in Chapter Three that it is the ego or 'self' factor itself which is depleted and temporarily lost in depressive illness. If you can grasp the fact that the loss of your ego is not inevitable you will be in a far better position to hang on to your own essential being and win the fight against depersonalization. For a person who temporarily loses his ego factor, *is* depersonalized. There is nothing within him that is capable of positive response to the outside world. As we saw earlier the ego factor arises in a baby to help control and govern the primitive urges of the id so that all expended energy is directed towards the successful achievement of the required target or goal. It is very much a positive psyche factor directed towards the ultimate good of the individual by enabling him both to fit into the context of his surrounding environment, and derive the greatest possible amount of reward and satisfaction for efforts made.

Loss of ego disturbs the normal state of dynamic equilibrium which exist when all three factors, id, ego and super-ego are functioning as they should. If the ego is lost there remains only the id, which is the swirling mass of instinctive urges, on the one hand and the super-ego, which is the conscience or moral principle, on the other. With no ego to bridge the gap between these two and establish harmonious co-operation it is not surprising that the net result, so far as the depressed person is concerned, is one of loss of self-esteem and guilt. The instincts of self-preservation and procreation are in existence, tempered only by the inhibiting restrictions of moral dictates. So the psychic energy represented by the urge towards self-preservation becomes negatively geared towards self-destruction and the psychic energy represented by sexual impulses becomes a subconscious source of anxiety, guilt and self-condemnation at the conscious level.

The second great advantage of seeing your depressive illness in perspective is that it enables you, between bouts of depression, to make a list of the signs and symptoms that occur as forerunners of an attack. Although ten randomly chosen depressed patients will experience this illness with ten different degrees of severity, nevertheless each individual has his or her particular 'prodromal phase'. One person will notice, for instance, that his sleep pattern tends to become disturbed and this is followed by a loss of sexual feeling, inertia and a tendency to burst into tears. Another may find, on the other hand, that fatigue and headaches more often prelude her depressive phases, coupled with bouts of irritation and great anxiety. A third, in contrast to both of these, may get attacks at regular six monthly intervals which are always preceded by profound loss of self-confidence, guilt about sexual feelings and a tendency to cry incessantly.

Holding on firmly to your ego principle, and being on the look out for (although not preoccupied by the thoughts of) the usual signs that a bout of depression threatens, are effective ways of preventing an attack or at least aborting it in its early phases.

I now intend to examine the physical treatment of depressive illness, in other words, drug therapy and ECT (electroconvulsive therapy). I have said already that I am writing this book because I do not think that orthodox medicine has the right approach or provides the right answer to treating depression. Why then am I bothering to discuss what it has to offer? Basically, because to be able to put the self-help methods I have devised into practice you naturally need a certain amount of motivation. The mildly and moderately depressed person often still has a vestigial sense of purpose in life, but the greater the degree of depression the greater the corresponding loss of motivation. So the methods I have devised, and will be discussing in the rest of the book, are ideal if you are between bouts of illness, or only suffering from a moderate degree of it. I consider medical methods to be appropriate only to the severely depressed person, but since this book is intended for all depressed people and their friends it is necessary to discuss these orthodox treatments.

Medical Treatment

Whether or not a depressed person should be hospitalized depends very much on the way in which his illness affects him. Doctors rarely entertain any doubts about whether or not to hospitalize a patient who either admits to thoughts about self-injury and self-destruction or whom the doctor strongly suspects is doing so secretly; likewise, the patient who lives alone, has no-one to care for him and is so affected by inertia, apathy and fatigue that he is unable to look after himself. Both types of patient clearly needs skilled medical care, as indeed does the individual who requests a spell in hospital because his degree of mental suffering is becoming intolerable.

Generally speaking, however, for reasons that will become apparent in the coming chapters, I avoid wherever possible sending depressed people into hospital. Although conditions in psychiatric hospitals and the psychiatric wards of general hospitals have improved vastly since the beginning of the century, no-one can deny that the number of patients admitted each year far exceeds the time and the resources that hospital staff have to give them. In addition to the inevitable lack of sufficient individual attention there is also a regrettable tendency, in some hospitals where overcrowding is a particular problem, to group together in open wards patients suffering from a number of different mental conditions. People with acute anxiety neurosis and severely depressed people, for example, both needing space, tranquillity and a freedom from stress, may well find themselves cheek-by-jowl with chronic schizophrenic patients who have become intensely institutionalized over many years in the same hospital. And grouping neurotic with psychotic patients — that is, the sick but essentially sane with severely disturbed patients who have lost all contact with reality — can have a very deleterious effect on the former.

Weekly or monthly appointments at the psychiatric out-patients department of a hospital can be beneficial to certain patients if the psychiatric registrar or consultant can spend a minimum of fifteen to twenty minutes with each patient. This ensures that chronically depressed people with no friends or relations to care for them, and few social contacts, can at least be certain of a sympathetic ear when they attend hospital. Fifteen to twenty minutes is not very long to carry out a course of psychotherapy — subdivided, as it is bound to be, into weekly or even monthly visits — but being listened to and given verbal reassurance of a supportive kind can benefit moderately depressed patients for a limited time. The problem is, however, that few patients see their psychiatrists for longer than ten minutes per interview and are liable to leave after their time is up with a prescription for another month's supply of antidepressants and a hurried word of comfort.

There is little, if anything, to be gained by the repeated administration of antidepressant tablets which may, in my view, severely hinder the patient's return to health. As I mentioned before, my own policy is to prescribe an antidepressant agent for very depressed patients with the object of raising their spirits sufficiently for them to be able to benefit from drugless therapy. Let's take a look at the various drugs that are prescribed for patients and establish what benefits, if any, they confer.

First, *antidepressant compounds*. There are three main types of these, the first being the tricyclics. Examples of these are imipramine (*Tofranil*), amitriptyline (*Trypizol*), nortriptyline (*Motival*), desipramine (*Pertofran*). All tricyclic antidepressant drugs act by blocking the re-uptake of noradrenaline at adrenergic nerve terminals. Some also block the re-uptake of 5-hydroxytryptamine (serotonin). In order fully to understand this you could refresh your memory by turning to the relevant section in Chapter Four. We saw that according to the Bio-amine theory of brain function (still known as such but now an established fact), serotonin and the catecholamines are essential for the transfer of mood and thought messages throughout the cerebral hemispheres. A deficiency of either impedes the power of thought, slows down mental function and considerably dampens the mood. A prolonged deficiency of either or both, can cause severe depression and it is this deficiency that the antidepressant drugs seek to reverse.

The deficiency concerned is a functional one and may be brought about by a variety of factors. One of these is, of course, insufficient neurotransmitter, in particular serotonin or noradrenaline, being produced at the synaptic nerve terminals for the transfer of nerve impulses when required. Another means by which a functional deficiency can be brought about, is excessively rapid uptake at the receiving synaptic nerve endings, where the molecules of neurotransmitter are immobilized too rapidly for their supply to maintain the required concentration. Thus, a thought impulse would reach the end of neurone A, granules of stored noradrenaline or serotonin would be released when the impulse arrived at the synaptic gap, and the message would be transferred to the beginning of neurone B. However, if the factors that attract the neurotransmitter at the beginning of neurone B are excessively active, the molecules of noradrenaline or serotonin would get 'grabbed' before transferring the nerve impulse effectively; consequently the impulses would have difficulty in crossing the synaptic gap. Tricyclic drugs work by blocking the excessively rapid uptake of noradrenaline at the synaptic nerve terminals. This restores, or helps to restore, the synaptic concentration of neurotransmitter to normal levels.

Side-effects of the tricyclic compounds include a dry mouth, constipation, blurred vision and a rapid heartbeat. A sudden fall in blood-pressure on rising from the sitting position, causing temporary dizziness can occur, and high doses of the drug can cause a pronounced tremor (trembling hands). Urinary retention (the inability to pass water) is also an established side-effect and the drugs are not considered suitable for patients with enlarged prostate glands, who already have a tendency to this complaint. Excessive sweating is also a fairly common effect although the mechanism of this response is not known. Weakness and fatigue often occur and a headache is fairly common, as are nausea and, occasionally, vomiting. Patients differ markedly in their response to these drugs, some suffering many side-effects and some hardly any. Older patients in particular tend to suffer from dizziness, low blood-pressure, constipation, urinary problems and trembling hands. Use of these drugs has also been associated with irregularities of the heartbeat and with cardiac failure, the latter usually occurring in patients with a predisposition to heart disease.

High doses of imipramine are sometimes known to trigger *grand mal* seizures, even in patients without a history of convulsions.

This drug can also produce an allergic type of obstructive jaundice which clears when the drug is discontinued, and the number of white cells in the blood can fall significantly as part of the same reaction. Skin rashes appear occasionally and photo-sensitization can occur, meaning that the skin of the patient on this particular antidepressant is badly affected by ordinary daylight. Quite apart from the fact that the tricyclic antidepressants have obviously toxic side-effects, their treatment of depressive illness is symptomatic, that is they do nothing to relieve the underlying condition or solve the problem of why it occurs. Both of these points are equally applicable to the next group of drugs, and constitute sufficient reasons for courses of either to be of short duration only.

The other large group of commonly prescribed

antidepressant compounds are the monoamine-oxidase inhibitors (known as the MAOIs). These inhibit the action of the enzyme responsible for breaking down those neurotransmitters which conduct mood and feeling impulses. In contrast to the tricyclic compounds, which function by blocking the over-speedy re-uptake of noradrenaline at the synaptic nerve terminals, the MAOIs prevent the breakdown of these amines specifically by counteracting the effect of the enzyme monoamine-oxidase.

There is no doubt about the effectiveness of the MAOIs in relieving depression in many patients. In fact, in common with some of the tricyclics, they can cause a state of mania, or hypomania, so that the patient is as excited, overstimulated or overactive, having taken the drug, as he was slow, dull and lethargic prior to treatment. The production of mania is one of the toxic side-effects of the MAOIs and they are also known for their other, more dangerous, side-effect, called the 'cheese reaction'. Certain foodstuffs, including cheese, broad beans, pickled herrings, red wine, beer, yeast, chicken liver, coffee and canned figs all contain an appreciable amount of a substance called tyramine. A patient given MAOI drugs has rigorously to avoid these items, for sudden episodes of dangerously high blood-pressure can result. This is thought to come about because the MAOIs inhibit monoamine-oxidase in the liver, as well as in the brain, and the tyramine which would normally be broken down by oxidative de-amination escapes this process and freely releases the noradrenaline, which is then present in above normal amounts in the nerve endings. The effect is a sudden and acute rise in blood-pressure, which causes palpitations, flushing, nausea and an agonizing headache, and may provoke a heart attack or stroke in a susceptible patient.

Besides the hyperexcitability and the 'cheese effect', MAOIs include the following among their toxic side-effects; tremors, insomnia and excessive perspiration, confusion and hallucinations, convulsions, a fall in blood-pressure on rising, dizziness, vertigo, poor sexual response, urinary retention, weakness, fatigue, blurred vision, a dry mouth and skin rashes.

MAOI therapy is also incompatible with several other forms of therapy, including amphetamines, certain pain-killing drugs, tricyclic antidepressants, anti-Parkinson drugs and certain forms of anaesthesia. MAOIs in common use are, isocarboxazid *(Marplan)*; ipronaizid *(Marsilid)*; phenelzine *(Nardil)*; and tranylcypromine *(Parnate)*.

When discussing the drug therapy of depression we must mention L-tryptophan, to which I referred earlier. There has been a considerable amount written in the Press about this substance in the recent past — it is a naturally occurring amino acid, which means that it is present in a number of food substances, normally included in our diet, and it can be useful in depression because it is a forerunner (what chemists call a 'precursor') of 5-hydroxytryptomine (serotonin). As discussed, the tricyclic antidepressants help depression by inhibiting the re-uptake of amine neurotransmitters (both noradrenaline and serotonin) and the MAOIs help the condition by combatting the enzyme responsible for breaking these two substances down.

L-tryptophan represents an approach to the problem from another angle; that is, supplying one of the substances known to be lacking in the brain of depressed people. Serotonin itself does not readily enter the brain, but L-tryptophan does and, being a precursor, is\ converted into serotonin within the substance of the brain matter, thus supplying extra quantities of serotonin where it is lacking at the synaptic gaps.

Since it is known that, when serotonin is synthesized from its precursor, MAOI drugs are able to potentiate its functional activity, combination therapy has recently been tried using L-tryptophan and a new MAOI inhibitor called selegiline *(Eldepryl)*, which lacks the dangerous 'cheese effect'.

The controversy aroused by L-tryptophan, was based on the question as to whether it should be made freely available to people to buy over the counter from health food shops and chemists. It is currently available on prescription as either *Optimax* or *Pacitrom* and, besides doubtlessly genuine concern for the public's welfare, there may well have been some concern on the part of the pharmaceutical companies, since patients can receive the same treatment as they offer in these two drugs, merely by buying a health supplement additive; thereby rivalling their sales to chemists and hospitals.

This issue aside, the problem is a difficult one because it is hard to know where to draw the line. Where does a food supplement cease to be just that and become a drug? Can a naturally-occurring substance be justifiably named a drug at all? The problem is not yet solved but L-tryptophan remains on sale and I will later be discussing the use of this amino acid as part of a combined approach to depressive illness.

Lastly, we must mention the use of sedatives (or anti-anxiety drugs) and hypnotic compounds (compounds that induce sleep). Many sedative drugs (commonly known as tranquillizers) are used for psychiatric illnesses. This includes depressive illness but, to my mind and in the opinion of many doctors who treat depressed people, sedative compounds have virtually no part whatever to play in the treatment of depressed people. Two widely prescribed sedative drugs are diazepam *(Valium)* and chlordiazepoxide *(Librium)*. Even when there is a high level of anxiety associated with depressive illness, it is by far better to avoid the use of these compounds altogether. Both of them, and compounds like them, dampen the mood to an even lower level, and *Valium* is known to exert a positively depressing effect on patients. The antidepressant drugs themselves exert what is known as an anxiolytic effect, that is they diminish the level of current anxiety. This is another reason for prescribing a short course of antidepressants for the severely depressed patient and withholding sedative therapy.

The same rationale underlies my attitude to hypnotic compounds, such as *Mogadon* (nitrazepam); *Halcion* (triazolam) and *Euhypnos* (temazepam). Used correctly, antidepressant drugs will correct insomnia, but most patients feel heavy and tired the following day after using a hypnotic the night before, regardless of the manufacturer's claims that their products are broken down and dealt with by the patient's metabolism overnight, thereby making morning sleepiness impossible.

It is worth saying a word or two here about the treatment of mania, since we mentioned this disturbance in the section in which manic-depressive psychosis was discussed. This illness can be what is known either as unipolar or bipolar. Unipolar illness is characterized by recurrent episodes of either mania or depression — never both. Bipolar illness, on the other hand, is featured by recurrent episodes of both mania and depression. Unipolar manic disorders are rare, and the bipolar disorders do not necessarily involve an alternation of two mood states. It is important always to be certain of the diagnosis, particularly since the differential diagnosis (or most likely alternative) is a form of schizophrenia characterized by mood alteration. This is because lithium — which is used to treat mania and its less severe form, hypomania — is ineffective in schizophrenia. Lithium carbonate *(Calcolit)* should not be regarded as a wondercure for all forms of cyclical mental illness — as once claimed — but it is effective in the treatment of the manic phase of manic-depressive illness; as a mood-stabilizing drug when used chronically in manic-depressives; and also as an anti-depressant in an ill-defined group of patients.

With respect to its action on the central nervous system, it would appear that lithium's therapeutic effects in manic-depressive illness are due to the properties it possesses in direct contrast to the standard antidepressant drugs. Instead of increasing available serotonin and noradrenaline, it encourages the re-uptake of noradrenaline, thereby diminishing the total available amount, and it increases the synthesis and the turnover rate of serotonin. The turnover rate is the speed at which this compound is metabolized, broken down and excreted from the body, to be replaced by a fresh supply. Lithium also has a number of actions which have not yet been determined, which account for its antidepressant effects.

Electro Convulsive Therapy (ECT)

The idea of ECT is alarming to many people. It is used in the treatment of very severe depression and can alleviate the symptoms dramatically. Two main problems pertain to its use. One of these is that the depressive illness generally recurs after a period of time and the other is that, since complete agreement has not yet been reached with respect to the way it works, there is no way of telling the extent of any damage that may occur to the brain substance, as a side-effect of the benefits. Nowadays, the 'convulsive' part of the name of this therapy is a misnomer for, although a convulsion like an epileptic seizure used to occur as a result of the small electric shock applied to the skull, nowadays a light anaesthetic and a muscle relaxant are given as a preliminary, and these suppress the convulsion while preserving the useful effects on the brain cells.

The treatment can be administered on an inpatient or day-patient basis. The only prerequisite for the day-patient is that he has neither eaten nor drunk since midnight the night before. The whole procedure takes a matter of minutes and relief from the symptoms of depression can occur after the first treatment session but are more likely to occur after the third or fourth. The number of treatment sessions depends on the view of the consultant psychiatrist about the suitability of the particular patient, and could vary from three to nine or ten.

As I have said, no research workers are as yet certain as to how depression is lifted as a result of a metal electrode being placed on either side of the skull and a small electric current being passed between them. An oversimplistic explanation is that the 'depressive' thought pathways are 'jolted' out of their undesirable pattern and caused to reform in such a way that the patient's mood is elevated. It is also thought that the passage of the electric current may alter brain amine metabolism, perhaps by increasing the supply of serotonin.

My own feelings about electro-convulsive therapy are ambivalent. I would never choose it as a first-line method of treatment, yet regard it as having a part to play in those few severely depressed patients who do not respond to a short sharp course of antidepressant therapy.

In the next chapter we will be taking a look at psychotherapy and the different methods used by psychotherapists for treating depression.

6.

PSYCHOTHERAPY

The essence of psychotherapy is a conversation — or series of conversations — which takes place between the therapist and the patient. The object of the therapist is to listen to the patient's problems, ask relevant questions about his past and his thoughts, feelings and desires, and help him to understand the cause, and the nature, of his present difficulties.

From the patient's point of view, successful psychotherapy can be likened to the opening of shutters and the drawing back of heavy curtains, allowing daylight and sunlight to reveal the contours of a room that hitherto has been in darkness.

The emotional turmoils, misery, confusion and sense of isolation that the patient in need of psychotherapy can experience, are in vivid contrast to his new views of himself and the world, once his problems have been shown to him in perspective. This is because the mental and emotional symptoms from which many patients suffer are in fact the unrecognized expression of feelings which have come about because of unpleasant associations with the past.

Two major forms of psychotherapy exist. There is *psychodynamic psychotherapy* on the one hand, based on Freud's work, teaching and development of psychoanalysis; and there is *behavioural psychotherapy* on the other, based on the application of learning theory and originating from the work of Pavlov on conditioned reflexes. The aim of the behaviour modification psychotherapist is to modify the patient's behaviour, or abnormal symptoms, which are seen as signifying an inability to adapt to situations, surroundings and lifestyle.

These bad behaviour patterns or 'bad habits' are thought to come about as inappropriate or undesirable reactions to past experience which have become habitual because they have not been corrected. The subconscious elements in motivation, such as the conflicts between ego, id and super-ego described by Freud, are not considered.

Essentially, behavioural psychotherapists pay more attention to the external behaviour of their patients and prefer the scientifically measurable data that can be amassed by the observation of outside appearances.

It is not possible, within the scope of this chapter, to consider fully both the psychodynamic school of psychotherapy and the behavioural school; we are here primarily concerned with the psychodynamic variety since, having followed the Freudian school of thought with respect to the development of depressive illness, it makes more sense to discuss the type of therapy that is derived from Freud's teachings and which is based upon a sound knowledge of his principles. If you believe, as I and many medically trained psychotherapists do, that early conflicts between the conscious and sub-conscious mind in infancy and childhood really *do* account for later mental disorders (or at least are a strong predisposing factor towards their development) you cannot, on the other hand, belong to the behavioural school of psychotherapy that takes no account of early inner turmoil.

Psychodynamic psychotherapy is known as such largely because it is founded upon the basic principles of dynamic interaction between the ego, id, and the super-ego. As I said earlier, normality implies a state of dynamic equilibrium between these three factors and in mental sickness there is, at least from the Freudian viewpoint, an observable shift in energy balance in one direction or another.

Psychodynamic Psychotherapy
It is important to remember that many of the inner conflicts

responsible for the later development of mental disorder (we will be referring exclusively to depressive illness in a moment) are forgotten about by the time the individual reaches adolescence or adulthood. Factors and situations may arise in his life which produce pronounced emotional upset and, although the reasons for his mental conflict, anxiety or depression lie in a parallel between the present situation and early conflict, this is likely to be anything but apparent to the mind of the sufferer. It is the role, therefore, of the psychotherapist, to create an empathy or rapport between himself and his patient whereby the truth can come to light so far as he is concerned, and be demonstrable and acceptable so far as the patient is concerned. The development of trust and confidentiality and, to my mind, although not often mentioned in textbooks, also of mutual liking, is all important.

With respect to the setting: the patient is made to feel as comfortable as possible, and the aim of the psychotherapist is to make the room in which he interviews patients as relaxing and aesthetically pleasing as possible. Hospital consultants rarely have a great deal of say with respect to how their consulting rooms are arranged, and none at all with respect to colour of paint, size of desk, or comfort afforded by armchairs or couch. However, most of them make every attempt to see that their patients are interviewed in as relaxing an environment as possible, and privately practising psychotherapists are free to decide on important factors such as colour scheme, furniture and the temperature of the room.

It is also worth mentioning here that the private practitioner is likely always to be able to offer his patients sessions lasting for at least one hour. Many patients in need of psychotherapy, whose only means of obtaining it is through the National Health Service, find that they are lucky if they receive fifteen to twenty minutes of the psychiatrist's undivided attention once a month.

Relaxation of the patient is essential if he is to start discussing intimate fears, and so a comfortable chair and analyst's couch are vital. The couch is usually so positioned that the head of the patient lying on it, is in front of the analyst's chair, so that the analyst is sitting behind him out of view. The doctor's desk and patient's chair are also generally arranged so that the patient sits to the side of the desk rather than directly opposite the doctor; as a large expanse of wood between the two can set up the feeling of an insurmountable barrier. With regard to the decoration of the room, many psychotherapists avoid portraying distinctly personal aspects of their private beliefs and lives. If, for example, a therapist adheres to a particular religion, plentiful evidence of religious conviction may well inhibit agnostic and atheistic patients. Some therapists deliberately have photographs of their wives, husbands or families on view, with the object of "damping down" the degree of transference (see later) that takes place from the patient to him or her. Others, however, avoid this, because the fantasies that can take place when transference occurs freely are often useful to the analyst in revealing patterns of the subconscious mind that he is trying to reach.

Supposing the patient is a man who for a long time has repressed homosexual feelings. Because of the intimate relationship, verbally, between himself and his therapist, he may start freely to fantasize that the therapist is homosexual and that the two of them are having a sexual relationship. Overt stress of the therapist's heterosexuality would be likely to repress these fantasies further and prevent them from coming to light.

Again, women who transfer certain images and personalities onto their therapist may well feel inhibited at the photograph of a beautiful wife and loving children. They may well feel left out and unable to form the transference that would in fact prove very beneficial.

Another objective of psychotherapists is to ensure that the time they give their patients is uninterrupted. Receptionists, secretaries or nurses knocking at the door, and telephones ringing, interrupt the concentration of both therapist and patient and can be calamitous in the case of a shy, reserved patient with little self-confidence, who is making tentative attempts to pour out his intimate secrets.

The following scenario is how a first interview would be conducted in ideal terms. Very often, of course — as happens in every day life — the psychotherapist is rushed for time, the patient is late or has a headache or an incapacitating attack of nerves, and neither side is as satisfied as he or she might be.

But in principle, first interviews would include the following points.

The psychotherapist reads the referral letter, or letters, sent to him in advance of seeing the patient, so that he is familiar beforehand with basic details such as name, nationality and nature of problem. Letters he would be likely to receive would be from the GP, if he is a psychiatrist who practices psychotherapy or from the GP and the consultant psychiatrist if he is a specialist in medical psychotherapy only. The receptionist is instructed to show the patient in as soon as he arrives and the psychotherapist greets him by name to make him feel at ease.

Seating the patient in a chair, placed as described earlier, the therapist then takes a history from the patient; despite the fact that he has already read details of the latter's difficulties. He does this because it is very valuable to hear patients give an account of their own problems in their own way. The GP, for example, may write a letter and say that he is referring a particular person because he is 'depressed'. However, such a term needs a great deal of further elucidation and a psychotherapist under those conditions would definitely ask the patient how long he had felt unwell, when he last remembered feeling really healthy and get him to describe, in his own time and in his own way, exactly what his own particular version of depressive illness amounted to. The therapist may well discuss the question of confidentiality. Ideally he will hear many details of the intimate thoughts and feelings that his patient entertains, and accounts of many past memories that may be acutely embarrassing to him. It is essential for the patient to feel both that he can talk with absolute confidence, and that the confidence will be respected at all times.

Psychotherapists should inform patients if they intend to discuss details of their case with other doctors. Few patients object and the ones that do generally acquiesce quite happily once they have had a brief meeting with the doctor or doctors who will be sharing the case study. The patient should also be reassured that nurses and ancillary workers will not have access to his case history and this can only be effected by the psychotherapist having sole access to files. Where this is possible it should be arranged.

Again, if the patient is completely against the idea of intimate details about himself being revealed to his general practitioner, in written form, the wish should be respected wherever possible. An appropriately informative letter, outlining the problems and treatment, can be written without the revelation of embarrassing details; alternatively the patient may agree to a phone call to his doctor revealing details which are not actually set down in writing. He must be equally reassured that friends, parents, husband or wife and other relations are not going to be contacted behind his back and his secrets discussed with them.

Many psychotherapists believe that the first interview should last only forty to fifty minutes, rather than twice as long, to avoid too many demands being made upon his own or the patient's concentration. Secondly, although most consultations of that nature work out to be roughly an hour, subsequent interviews should preferably take place at the same time and in the same location; occur two to three times per week, rather than once a week; and last for the same length of time as the initial interview. The idea of 'little and often' is a rough guide to success from the frequency point of view rather than two-hour interviews at sporadic times with no regularity or pattern to them.

Subsequent interviews will be characterized by the patient, rather than the doctor, taking the lead role. Some patients can talk about their problems volubly, others find it very difficult to get going. If the latter is the case, the therapist will probably help by not only inviting the patient to talk freely and at length but also prompting him with relevant questions such as 'What were you thinking, on the way to this consultation?', or 'Do you feel that you are being forced to come to see me against your will?' The second and subsequent interviews frequently take place with the patient lying supine on the couch facing away from the therapist, and the latter will often then try to set the patient's relevant thoughts in motion by using the technique of 'free association' — that is, inviting the patient to say anything at all that comes into his mind. This is often very difficult and the patient realizes for the first time that there is a great deal of his experience that he cannot put into words but which he can feel very strongly.

What commonly happens is that, when a patient is first confronted with the fact that a lot of past painful experience has been repressed, he tries to resist the emergence into his conscious mind and therefore into verbalization, of his inner turmoil. The therapist can overcome this problem in one of three ways. *Confrontation*, for example, 'You are denying your fear to me.' *Interpretation*, for example, 'You are afraid because I remind you of your father and you deny this because you have always sought to win your parent's affection by liking both of them.' Alternatively by *reconstruction,* for example, hypothetical historical statements of previously buried aspects of the patient's childhood past. For instance 'Your fear and suppression of it must parallel how you felt when you were little, your father and I representing your older brother, uncle. etc.'

It should be mentioned here that some therapists distinguish between 'psychoanalysis' proper and 'psychoanalytic psychotherapy'. The former is more intense and deep reaching, often necessitates three to five sessions a week between patient and analyst for several years, and invariably involves the patient in the supine position on the couch with the analyst sitting behind.

The psychotherapist, on the other hand, may or may not use the free association technique; is more likely to see the patient once or twice a week only, and will position himself facing the patient, both sitting in easy comfortable chairs a few feet apart. Psychoanalysis proper is by far the more demanding and intensive form of treatment and its only definable limit is when the patient has completely recovered, or recovered as much as is deemed possible. Psychotherapy is altogether less intensive but not necessarily less beneficial. Because most of this kind of treatment is available only from private practitioners, to continue psychoanalytic sessions at the rate of four or five per week, particularly when the sessions can cost between twelve and twenty-five pounds each, is clearly outside the scope of most people. For that reason psychoanalytic psychotherapy is considerably more widely practised. It is not feasible to go into a more detailed account of psychoanalytic psychotherapy in this book. Some of the techniques used, and a lot of the interpretations reached, may well seem bewildering or even absurd to people who have not studied the subject; but many good books can be found in bookshops and libraries and these are very helpful if you wish to know more about it. The following is a pertinent quote from *A Complete Guide To Therapy* by Joel Kovel (Pelican Books).

> The healing power of psychoanalysis lies then in the hoary dictum 'know thyself', not because such knowledge need be beneficial (it is often enough quite noxious) — but because the self which has succeeded to such knowledge is a self transformed, tempered, made supple, truer, a self that is master — in so far as one can be — of its internal forms.

Before we look at how psychotherapy can help depressive illness I will just say a word about 'transference'. Transference is an essential part of the therapeutic relationship between analyst or therapist and patient. Neurosis is essentially self-estrangement, resulting from a state of imbalance. Because there is so much self-alienation and frustrated desire in neurosis, therapy can do most for neurotic patients by offering some means of satisfying that desire. Two things are necessary for this to take place, there must be an object capable of gratifying the longing and this must clearly be permissible, a point which has to be made clear to the patient, because the desire would not have arisen in the first place if the patient had not experienced it as wrong and forbidden. Because these two functions can be fulfilled by one person in the patient's life, the therapist allowing him or herself to be considered as a love object to the patient, and permitting this kind of feeling to take place without remonstrance, often enables the therapy to get going easily and smoothly.

In the same way therapy can rapidly make some neurotic people feel a great deal less so by setting itself up in the patient's mind as a moral authority. Since the therapist defines what is right and wrong he gains transcendence over the damning power that has beset the patient in neurotic turmoil, thus relieving the pressure from within. In doing this it realigns the personality with society as a whole.

The feeling that the patient has for the therapist is not, however, always one of love and unfulfilled longing. What is happening at a subconscious level is a repetition of an earlier relationship in the current setting. So far as psychotherapy is concerned, transference is strictly definable, and the long term of treatment enables a transference parallel of the original infantile neurosis to take place towards the therapist and to be overcome.

Psychotherapy and Depression

Some therapists claim that the tendency to become depressed can, in all cases, be entirely abolished. Others attest that particular episodes of depression can be alleviated and the patient enabled to deal better with depression should it recur. We have seen that one of the most notable characteristics of depressive illness is lack of self esteem and we have seen how the origins of this can be traced back to the oral period when frustration of gratification due to interference from the external environment, including people other than mother, can cause bewilderment, resentment, frustration and rage-turned-inwards. The fact that the rage is directed at 'self', and feelings of worthlessness and self-abnegation become a set part of the personality, is due to the fact that insufficient love and attention are given to the child during this confusing period. The result is that the psyche of the depressed person becomes, and remains, extremely sensitive to events which may lower self esteem; reacting profoundly (it is worth remembering the all-or-nothing reaction) to circumstances which to normal people seem trivial.

Hence failure to pass an examination or a minor marital disruption can cause a profound depressive reaction. It is worth noting here that some depressed people say that it is only during depressive phases that they have a clear insight into their own nature and that the phases between depressive episodes are no more than false images. Certainly a phase of depression distorts the vision but this view is correct in the sense that a person with a depressive personality is either experiencing depression him or herself, or striving desperately to avoid an attack. This may be by overactivity (seen in a pronounced form in manic-depressive psychosis), or by attempting to win the approval of other people and gain respect and esteem from external sources. In that way the depressed person is right when he says that his state of depression is more truly a reflection of his inner being than his non-depressed state.

We should also remember that a dependence on approval from others, frequent success and triumphs, and constant reassurances of love, are essential to a depressed person.

The depressed person is also less than normally assertive with other people and generally extremely anxious to please them. He is in fact anxious above anything to avoid blame, and is not only supersensitive in his own feelings but also hyper-aware of those of others. Such a degree of adaptation has this disadvantage: that because the winning of approval is the *sine qua non* of existence, a person with a depressive personality is unlikely to be an effective leader or executive. He or she is too ready to defer to the opinion of other people which he automatically assumes is superior to his own. A natural development of this is an even further lowering of his own self-esteem; and an uncertainty about his own opinions and feelings. Being always guided by the opinions of others, he often ends up with no clearly defined opinion of his own.

Helplessness plays a large part in depression. Depressed people feel quite incapable of affecting the course of events and tend to give up and adopt a passive role. They feel that whatever choice they make is bound to be the wrong one and this increases the sense of helplessness for, above all, they wish to avoid incurring the disapproval of others.

Later in life, passivity is often replaced by ceaseless striving, but the achievement of the goal is often succeeded by a depressive phase. Normal people experience euphoria on completing a lengthy and demanding task and use the subsequent period to 'recreate' themselves. A depressed person, on the other hand, experiences a relapse — and conviction of his own ineffectiveness. All the time he is striving hard to attain a goal he can convince himself, temporarily, of his own worth and ability to cope. Achievement of the goal is followed by inertia, apathy, disappointment and depression.

All depressive people feel hostility, but it is an emotion which they suppress at all costs. You cannot tolerate repeated subjugation to the will of others, or constant deference to your inferiors, or the knowledge that you are unable to command respect (which you recognize as due to others in your situation and therefore possibly to you), without experiencing resentment. This constructive hostility could, of course, be made to work for the person and enable him or her to be more self-assertive and definite in his views, but it is repressed into a destructive form and works against him.

Having further outlined aspects of the depressive personality, it is now possible to summarize what the therapist is aiming at and see how positive results can be achieved. First, the fact that the therapist is prepared to go on seeing a depressed person regularly for a period of time helps to counteract his innate despair. Then, since the patient feels that at least one person, whom he likes and for whom he feels respect, really appreciates him, he may then start to feel that other people might be less critical than he had hitherto thought. Next, the therapist may be able to boost his patient's ego sufficiently for him to recognize his own effectiveness and success on many occasions. Finally, the therapist may reveal and put into action the aggressive side of the patient's personality so that he may be more constructively self-assertive.

With diligent history taking and with the use of a number of psychotherapeutic techniques, it is sometimes possible to elicit the actual instance in infancy or childhood which predisposed the individual's personality to depressive illness. Prolonged analysis can often reveal precipitating events, as can hypnoanalysis (analysis carried out under hypnosis) by a hypnotherapist. A good hypnotic subject can often be led back or 'regressed' to the stage in his early life at which the long-forgotten trauma took place. Often, evoking the memory and talking about it with the therapist will enable the patient to understand the reason for the various symptoms of depressive illness that he suffers. He will be able to understand why he lacks assertiveness, why he feels unworthy and inept, and why he feels incapable of commanding the respect of others. Such realization and understanding often have a highly therapeutic effect.

7.

YOUR PERSONAL PROGRAMME: THE PHYSICAL APPROACH

In this chapter, and the following two, I am going to discuss the three main aspects of the personal programme I have worked out over the number of years that I have spent helping people with depressive illness. So far we have taken a look at some of the factors that contribute to this condition and have noted that both a short bout of drug therapy and psychodynamic psychotherapy can help to alleviate the condition.

I made clear in the early part of this book that depression is not 'caused' by one factor or another but is what we call multifactorial, so that many aspects of the illness have to be taken into consideration for treatment to be effective. I have mentioned, too, the role that I see antidepressant drugs playing in a total treatment scheme; that is, the alleviation of the very severe form of the illness to enable the patient to co-operate with other forms of therapy.

When the patient *is* able to co-operate even a little, psychotherapy, if appropriate, is in a position to extend some help. I say if appropriate because the scheme I have devised is flexible and must be tailored to suit individual needs. Psychotherapy will work wonders for certain people suffering from depression yet do very little, if anything, to help others. A certain amount depends upon the personality of the patient concerned; on the rapport that is struck between him and the analyst or therapist and whether the necessary realization of repressed hostility, past emotional trauma in childhood etc., can successfully be bought into the field of his conscious awareness. Certainly the techniques designed to prompt the evolution of a successful therapeutic relationship are valid. But, just as penicillin does not cure all forms of chest infection, or even for that matter, all forms of chest infection caused by a bacteria susceptible to penicillin, so, likewise, psychotherapy cannot be regarded as a panacea for all neurotic ills.

I will be referring to the use of psychotherapy again in Chapter 8. I will just take this opportunity of pointing out that the importance I stressed earlier of being able to regard your depression in the same light as any other illness rather than a severe flaw warping your personality and mind, is reflected by the good effect psychotherapy has — by revealing the underlying psychological causes for symptoms. The dictum 'know yourself' applies equally to both these states of awareness.

The first phase of the self-help programme I have devised can be called the *physical approach*. As we have seen, depression is characterized by the partial, or complete, depletion of the psychic energy belonging to the ego factor. The greater the depletion, the less 'self' exists which is capable of experiencing pleasure, joy, hope and satisfaction. Hence, the more severe the depression the more inert and apathetic the patient becomes. Where ego depletion is almost total, the patient is, by definition, incapable of looking after himself and should either be hospitalized and treated with a short sharp burst of antidepressant medication or nursed carefully at home, visited regularly by his doctor and looked after by family or friends who realize the seriousness of the condition. I would only seek to hospitalize a patient who was bordering on a psychotic state and/or whom I suspected might be suicidal. Alternatively, I might choose to hospitalize someone whose precipitating factors to depressive illness were very clearly part and parcel of his home environment, and who would clearly benefit from removal to neutral territory.

Otherwise, I would suggest home nursing to be preferable, stressing to those concerned with looking after the patient that great patience and tolerance would be necessary. This would have particular reference to making certain that the patient invariably took his medication, and maintaining sufficient contact with him, despite his obvious wish to withdraw from human contact, for a clear picture to be retained of his state of mind.

Some severely depressed patients get a freak energy burst during an apparently very inert phase and, although they may appear apathetic and unresponsive, they may in fact be planning to take an overdose of their tablets, or to seek their own end in some other more violent way.

What do I mean by a short, sharp burst of antidepressant therapy? My first choice lies with the tricyclic antidepressants and I find myself, in these circumstances, frequently choosing clomipramine *(Anafranil)* because, not only is it a very effective antidepressant agent, but it also markedly diminishes the obsessional and phobic conditions which can accompany depression; as well as reducing the level of attendant anxiety. For an adult I normally start the treatment with 10 milligrams daily of *Anafranil* for three days, increasing the dose gradually until the patient is receiving 25 to 50 milligrams per day. This is effective in some people but not in others. Some require as much as 100 milligrams daily and, whatever the dose, it can be given either at breakfast-time, lunchtime and in the evening in divided doses, or as a single dose at night. (For an elderly patient I would start with an initial 10 milligrams per day; but would not exceed a maximum dose of 75 milligrams per day.)

Where the tricyclic compounds fail to alleviate symptoms, the MAOI antidepressants can often benefit a patient. I don't feel that there is a great deal to choose between these compounds but isocarboxazid *(Marplan)* is a commonly prescribed one, as is iproniazid *(Marsilid)*. Neither the tricyclic nor the MAOI drugs 'work' for the first seven to ten days of treatment. This is a disadvantage which they all share and one which sometimes sways the consultant's opinion in favour of ECT, which can often act a great deal more rapidly. During the first seven to ten days of therapy, the side-effects can be expected to show themselves; for example the patient may feel even more drowsy and inert than before — so much so that he can barely

keep awake. He may complain of a metallic taste in his mouth
and at the same time show signs of halitosis (bad breath). He
may also suffer from a stuffy nose, a mild headache and a dry
mouth.

I think it is worth mentioning here, and I must stress that
this is my own opinion only and in no way reflective of the
findings of recent research, that clomipramine *(Anafranil) can
work* a great deal more rapidly than the manufacturers claim
and most doctors find. I make no secret of the fact that I, too,
have suffered from severe depression in the past and probably
the reason for my lack of embarrassment in saying so is because
I have learnt to see it in the way that I have started you thinking
about it. That is, as a 'nuisance' complaint, or tendency, such
as a touch of rheumatism or recurrent migraine attacks which,
once coped with successfully, can be robbed of their ability
to cause you any real trouble.

My own depressive episodes, which started at the age of
eighteen and lasted on and off for some fifteen years, no doubt
stimulated my particular interest in the illness and in other
depressive patients. I *had* to work out a scheme, first of all for
helping myself and secondly for benefitting all those patients
suffering from the same complaint. I tried several different
tricyclic compounds for varying periods before a doctor friend
suggested that I try *Anafranil*. I chose a fairly high
commencement dose of 25 milligrams, which I took as a single
dose every night before going to sleep. I noticed a lightening
of mood and slight, but increasing abatement of symptoms from
the first morning after taking the initial dose, and the
improvement was maintained until my own brief course of
therapy came to an end and I was able to turn to other means
of coping with my illness.

Many people would say that this response was no more than
a placebo effect, that is a 'mind over matter' effect, which came
about because I believed that the drug was going to do me good.
This may well be so and I do not possess sufficient scientific
evidence to argue against this opinion, but since other equally
efficacious compounds had no effect whatever, even a placebo
one, this suggests to my way of thinking that part of my own
problem lay with a specific biochemical defect that

clomipramine is particularly good at rectifying.

As we have seen, if you take ten people who are suffering from depression, each will have a different series of factors which could precipitate this illness. Even for those who share the common factor of defective brain biochemistry — what we call the biochemical profile will be slightly different in each individual. One, for example, may make insufficient noradrenaline (see Chapter 4), the next depressed person may possess overactive enzymes capable of destroying the noradrenaline which he does make. The third depressed man or woman may make insufficient serotonin. I feel that this is the underlying explanation for any antidepressant compound working extremely well in certain individuals, such as clomipramine did in my case, and being ineffective in others.

My scheme for physical treatment proper starts, therefore, with a patient capable of making at least the minimum required response to the treatment offered. If I were to say that I could summarize the whole aspect of the physical approach to treatment, simply by the injunction 'keep active!' I would most likely evoke little more than disbelief and bewilderment from any reader who has suffered from depression him or herself. The one thing, as I have taken pains to point out, that you *cannot* do when you feel depressed is to partake in any kind of voluntary activity. We saw in the discussion of psychotherapy that people with a depressive personality often learn the trick of coping both socially and in the context of their job. I am here using the word 'socially' in its narrowest sense, to include the daily expected verbal intercourse with friends, relations and colleagues. People in all these categories may be convinced, by the depressed person's successful veneer, that he or she is a cheerful, sympathetic, nice sort of person who readily listens and sympathizes, is capable of managing his or her job and has a happy disposition. It often takes someone very close to the depressed person to know that, underneath, they are angry, hostile and extremely unhappy. Certainly, people whom I would classify as severely depressed *cannot* cope, but those who are moderately depressed can generally do so, and we will see in a moment how this can be beneficial.

What does a person suffering from depression want? He

doesn't *want* anything, because the ability to expect pleasure, enjoy it and desire more is lacking in him; but, using the word 'want' rather differently, the person sick with depression will often state that all he wishes for is oblivion. Darkness, silence, warmth, physical comfort, and a total lack of any form of external stimulation. No telephones ringing, nobody interfering with him — even to ask if he is feeling better — no-one offering food or drink, information or conversation, stimulation or amusement. He or she wishes to be absolutely free from any form of commitment, involvement or responsibility, and wishes only for peace, which is seen as a complete and continuing absence of contact with the things and the people that go to compose an everyday environment.

It struck me some years ago that this mental withdrawal from the external environment is similar to withdrawal — or should I say regression — to the foetal state. The unborn baby is warm, quiet, comfortable, protected and fed his necessary nourishment in a way that enables him to remain completely passive. My own theory is that one of the factors in a depressed person's wish for a similar condition to that of the unborn child is a subconscious wish to return to the pre-infantile condition, because deeply inbedded in his subconscious mind is the awareness that a number of his problems took place in infancy and childhood. A return to, and simulation of, the foetal state represents a subconscious urge to go back to the whole, healthy and untraumatized condition in which the foetal psyche was as yet unharmed by external factors.

It is easy to see, when you consider all the benefits the unborn child has, why being born is such a severely traumatic experience. I am not necessarily suggesting that the trauma undergone at that time has a lastingly deleterious effect; although disciples of the Leboyer method of delivery suggest that there are many benefits to be gained from arranging for a warm, dark, peaceful environment, possibly with soft music playing, as the baby's first contact with the outside world. Be that as it may I feel there is a lot to be said for Leboyer's ideas. Being propelled out of the womb and into the cold light of day must, under any circumstances, come as a tremendous shock to the baby's system. Instead of darkness there is light; instead of moist warmth there is the relatively cold, dry, external air; instead of silence or muffled sounds there is the cold clank of instruments and the loud voices of the nursing staff and midwives. The shock of the severing of the vital umbilical cord, that has been literally a lifeline for forty weeks, is incalculable.

Then there is the unpleasant sensation of being touched, held, picked up and (if the baby is unlucky) held unceremoniously upside down, suspended by the heels, and smacked on the bottom to make it cry. Worst of all must be that sudden, and probably agonizing, first breath in which the lungs expand to receive the vital but foreign mixture of atmospheric gases which it will continue to breathe for the rest of its life. It is no wonder that excessive or rough stimulation at the time of birth can result in a tendency to neurotic illness later in life.

Using the same parallel, it is *extremely painful* for the depressed person to submit him or herself to any unnecessary source of stimulation, but this is what Anthony Storr has to say for the value of stimulation in people suffering from depression:

> Nearly all episodes of depression resolve themselves 'spontaneously'. I have put the word 'spontaneously' into inverted commas, because close examination of such recovery usually discloses psychological factors of a more or less subtle kind which have prompted recovery, just as close examination discloses precipitants of the attack, and these factors seem to be of three kinds. First the patient, especially if he is managing to remain at work, may find that his self-esteem is partially restored by discovering that he can be effective at it. Most jobs require repeated actions of some kind which do not demand weighty decisions or new initiatives; and the fact that a depressed person finds to his surprise that he can continue to function effectively at this level may convince him that he is not entirely useless. That is why I seldom reinforce a depressed person's desire to 'give up' and retire to bed or to hospital unless he is exhibiting clear psychotic symptoms, is dangerously suicidal, or is so depressed that he cannot co-operate.

Do not ever feel despair at your apparent total lack of 'lifeforce', joy, reactibility etc., if you suffer from periods of depression yourself, nor if you are married to, or otherwise related to, someone else who suffers in this way. The ego and therefore the 'self' principle may well be thoroughly depleted; but the vital faculties are still safe within, only waiting for the right kind of stimulus to awaken them.

What I suggest to my depressed patients is that, instead of withdrawing into themselves and retiring from all but the most essential contact with those around them, they seek the exact opposite; that is, they literally bombard themselves with as many excitatory stimuli as they can absorb. Clearly, at least in the early stages, a person affected by depression will be unable to do much of this for himself. Someone who cares for him will have to 'get him going', so to speak, and see that he keeps to a regular routine, a very difficult task indeed for the patient will initially show every resistance to so painful an experience. When patients require this kind of therapy and they have no-one to help them to follow it, sometimes the best that I can offer is an appointment with me seven days a week, to give them some focal point within the day which will act as their directive for the next twenty-four hours, and boost their self-esteem because they have been successful in adhering to a plan.

This therapy can be likened to the intensive external stimulation of deeply comatose individuals which often has such beneficial effects. We quite often read in the newspapers nowadays of children, men and women who have been the victim of some kind of accident that has inflicted severe head injury; and of the determination of the parents, husband, or wife to awaken the unconscious victim, thus enabling recovery to take place. Their persistent and dogged efforts often succeed, simply because the brain is at last stimulated into activity and the shaking off of unconsciousness, by repeated bombardment with auditory and tactile stimuli. A person close to the unconscious person repeats his or her name, plays music familiar to them and even recorded voices of childhood playmates or colleagues at work. And the patient's arms and legs are flexed and extended over and over again, day after day — the reward in many cases being the slow but gradual regaining of conscious awareness.

The manner in which repeated physical activity, preferably of a vigorous and stimulatory nature, can help a patient suffering from depression is partly by means of the release of the adrenaline hormones from the adrenal glands. It is known that inactivity and inertia are almost invariably present in depressive illness; it has recently been suggested that one of the precipitating causes of depression may well be long term inactivity and a sedentary lifestyle. Referring to the biogenic amine theory and the important part noradrenaline, or the lack of it, plays in mood disorders, it is interesting to note that both noradrenaline and adrenaline are released into our bloodstream whenever we are confronted with a challenging situation.

The release of adrenaline and noradrenaline is part of the primitive reflex mechanism which enables mammals to cope with a threatening situation by 'flight or fight'. A sudden shock, a fright, an unexpected noise, the sudden appearance of an enemy, releases these hormones into the bloodstream and the muscles of the body are primed to a state of maximum activity. Respiration becomes rapid and shallow; the heart beats very rapidly; the mouth tends to dry; the pupils of the eyes dilate; and the organism is 'set up' to deal with whatever situation it is encountering.

At the same time, of course, supplying noradrenaline to the bloodstream in large amounts inevitably means that the blood supply to the brain will similarly conduct large quantities of noradrenaline to its tissues, and a pronounced lightening of mood can be expected to follow.

The key to the secret is stimulation of the mid-brain. We have discussed the bio-amine neurotransmitters and how they act in the processes of thought, mood and feeling in the upper regions of the cerebral hemispheres. It is in particular the fore-brain or front area of the hemispheres that is most concerned with these functions, and when this is precipitated into a state of depression, abnormal controlling messages are sent from this area to the mid-brain which, as we saw earlier, is also intimately concerned with control of mood, sexual impulse and muscular activity. The mid-brain (or hypothalamus) is in addition the control centre for the mechanisms of sleep and appetite, and this helps to explain why these functions are badly affected symptomatically by depressive illness. Depression occurring in the fore-brain effectively places a check on mid-brain function and, for psychological health to be maintained at a biochemical or organic level, an active hypothalamus, or mid-brain, is vital.

Harmony can be restored, and the correct balance maintained between the cerebral hemispheres and the mid-brain, by increasing the blood levels of adrenaline and noradrenaline. As we have seen, the tricyclic and MAOI antidepressants help to do this for us, but we do not, as an every day practice have to swallow drugs in order to bring this about. Daily deliberate vigorous activity can do the job just as well and in a much more healthy way.

Although we explain all I've been discussing nowadays in terms of brain function and biochemistry, actual awareness of the benefits that can accrue from physical activity to people in a melancholic state, is not new. In the last century in Bavaria, Father Sebastian Kneipp, famous in the history of modern hydrotherapy, approached depression with a demanding course of cold water baths and outdoor exercise. He speaks in his handbook *My Water Cure* of the benefits two depressed students received when they came to him in the Easter holidays with symptoms of acute misery, headaches, sleeplessness and excessive tiredness:

> As it was springtime, and the ground still moist and tolerably cold, I gave them the advice to spend their holidays walking barefoot in the woods and meadows, with rapid exercise whenever they felt cold; also from time to time to stand or walk about for two or three minutes in a stream or ditch filled with water. In like manner they were told to put their arms completely in water two or three times daily.

They were sufficiently invigorated to return to their colleges with renewed enthusiasm for work, finding studying a great deal easier than before and looking forward to another opportunity of undergoing this bracing regimen.

Sharing a common basis with this idea, are the frantic and vigorous voodoo dances designed to chase out the demons of melancholia; the infliction of pain by means of a sound whipping which in medieval times was designed to drive out evil spirits; and the deliberate adoption of an exciting and stimulating occupation, which Samuel Johnson maintained to Boswell, invariably overcame lethargy. He told the latter that the best advice for a melancholic man was as follows: 'Let him take a course in chemistry, or a course of rope dancing, or a course of anything to which he is inclined.' This indicates that another way of stimulating our mid-brain, besides that of physical activity, is that of taking up a diverting and interesting new pastime.

The secret of successfully altering your lifestyle to one that is far less conducive to depression is to devise a personal plan between depressive phases and put it into motion so that it may stave off any tendency that depressive illness shows to recurrence. In that way a slight fall in buoyancy of feelings or any other of the prodromal symptoms that you may personally experience will then act as a signal for you to adhere even more closely to a regimen that includes the following: exercise, rest, work, recreation, adequate sleep, a good diet, some time spent alone each day to enable you to unwind, and simple activities/pastimes/hobbies. I will set out the details of a day to day programme, with slight individual variations, that I have used for some years for people suffering from recurrent depression. It has proved highly effective and was no less so in my case, for I made myself the first guinea pig upon which to try my plan.

- A cold bath every morning.
- Attendance as usual at your place of work; or school, college, university etc., if you are studying.
- One half-hour spent every single day performing some kind of aerobic exercise, such as jogging (which can be on the spot indoors in bad weather), swimming, dancing, cycling, skating or playing squash. It doesn't matter what you choose. There are two essentials to bear in mind: the first is that whatever activity you choose must make you breathe more rapidly, make your pulse increase in speed and, most important, make you feel physically tired by the time you finish.

  The second essential, is that you choose an activity you *enjoy*.

- Some music to be listened to every single day, (radio,

cassette or tape recorder, it doesn't matter which). Choose anything you like that is *rousing*. The choice I recommend is brass band music. If you loathe this, choose something else, but there is something in military music played with swing and gusto by a brass band that stirs our noble, if hidden, feelings and sets the toes of many listeners involuntarily tapping the floor in time with the music.

● Incense sticks to be burnt; these are obtainable from shops that sell Indian and Eastern goods, and from markets. Choose something pungent, stimulating and strongly smelling; something that makes you very aware of its presence and makes you feel good to breathe it in, and smell it. My own favourites for therapeutic purposes are musk, amber and frangipani. You may prefer the more traditional perfumes of rose, sandlewood or patchouli. A particularly stimulating combination is to burn a stick of amber with one either of musk or of frangipani. Place them at the same point in the room, then you will get the full benefit from the mingled perfumes.

● Your diet should be attended to, from two particular points of view. Aim for a wholefood diet that is nutritionally sound, and avoid, as far as possible, the use of any foodstuffs containing artificial colouring matter, preservatives and flavourings. I was horrified to learn the statistics with respect to colouring matter consumption per head annually in the U.K. Each of us, on average, consumes a kilogram every year of artificial food dye alone. This means that people who rely on convenience foods and processed items consume a great deal more than this, for there is a growing trend among many towards wholefood diets, which exclude the use of any such material.

● 'Looking and seeing' should be practised for five minutes three times a day. It is an easy and rewarding exercise and it is possible to do it anywhere apart from in the total dark. Take five minutes off from whatever you are doing and concentrate your gaze on several objects in the room around you, one after the other, allowing your eyes to become accustomed to the shape, size, visual texture and colour of each item, concentrating really hard when you do so and filling your mind with the details of what you are seeing. Work out, roughly, the dimensions of the object. Choose a verbal expression to describe the colour and texture, and when you have performed this exercise close your eyes for half a minute afterwards and recall the various objects, practising until you can summon up their exact images.

Choose simple objects initially, a glass of water, a vase with a single flower in it, a coloured plate or a piece of ribbon or string.

If you are outside, carry out the exercise in exactly the same way, providing of course that you are not driving a car, for overpreoccupation with any one or a small number of objects can distract your attention from the overall road conditions.

You will see from the programme I have sketched out so far that exercise is recommended both for the body and for the brain; and that the five senses are also deliberately stimulated on a regular daily basis. The cold bath stimulates your tactile sense and acts also as a shock to the system, thereby getting the adrenaline mobilized for the day. The cheerful band music playing marches, foxtrots and quicksteps, stimulates your sense of hearing; what you choose to eat (and this should take two factors into consideration, nutrition and appeal) will stimulate your sense of taste and the incense sticks will arouse your sense of smell. 'Looking and seeing' stimulates your visual faculties.

In contrast to your innate desire to protect yourself from unnecessary stimuli, you are in fact deliberately bombarding your five senses in a pleasant and constructive way. The cold bath or shower, the physical exercise and the bracing music should all excite you and increase your blood levels of adrenaline and noradrenaline. The stimulation of your other senses will gradually become pleasant to you and thereby prevent a further withdrawal of energy from your ego factor. Before going on to the next chapter, which is the second part of your personal plan, I will give you details of a wholefood diet.

Wholefood Diet

Wholefoods are foods that have had nothing added and nothing taken away. They are neither processed nor refined, and contain no artificial additives. Wholemeal bread, made from unrefined flour still containing B vitamins and minerals, is whole food. Sliced white, plastic wrapped bread is junk food. A wholefood diet emphasizes fresh fruit and vegetables, preferably organically or compost grown, eaten either raw or lightly cooked. It supplies fibre; vitamins and minerals; and proteins, carbohydrate and fat in the right proportions. It emphasizes the use of cold-pressed vegetable oils and the necessity for a low intake of salt, sugar and animal fat.

Breakfast: Make sure you eat this meal. Choose wholegrain-based breakfast cereals, wholemeal bread, yogurt, fresh fruit juice or fresh or dried fruit. A free-range boiled or poached egg can be added from time to time.

Lunch: (Which can be swapped if necessary with the evening meal.) A good choice is homemade soup with fresh vegetables. A salad made with leaf and root vegetables, sprouted seeds, nuts, cereal grains and other seeds such as sesame and pumpkin.

Evening Meal: The protein part of this meal should consist of lean meat, fish, poultry, cheese or free-range eggs, or a combination of two of the three plant proteins found in pulses, grains and nuts. The grains include pasta and pastry made with wholemeal flour (for example as used in pies, tarts and flans), and the pulses include the wide variety of lentils, peas and beans now available in supermarkets and health food shops, which can be made into delicious pâtés, hot or cold salads and roasts. The protein should be served with a raw vegetable salad or lightly boiled or steamed vegetables. Green leafy vegetables should be eaten at least once a day. Good desserts for a wholefood diet are fresh fruit, live yogurt or low-fat cheesecake, crumbles, pastries, mousses or pancakes. Drinks should aim at a moderate amount of alcohol, if taken at all, and show a preference for natural mineral water. Freshly squeezed fruit and vegetable juices, herb teas, coffee substitute and decaffeinated coffee, as well as yeast extract drinks, are also most beneficial.

Finally, it is a very good idea to supplement your diet with organically produced supplements. I recommend a reliable multi-vitamin compound, and a multi-mineral one as well. I also suggest taking 1 gram, morning and evening, of Vitamin

C; two capsules of ginseng a day; vitamin B_3 (niacin), 100 milligrams twice daily; vitamin B_6 (pyridoxine), 50 milligrams three times a day; and dolomite (or bonemeal tablets), to supply calcium, which should yield 300 milligrams three times daily. The dolomite will at the same time supply magnesium which has a beneficial effect in calming symptoms of anxiety.

L-tryptophan can be used, (page 63) preferably under the guidance of a doctor or therapist. A dose that suits many people is two 500mg tablets taken after the evening meal.

8.

YOUR PERSONAL PROGRAMME: LEARNING TO COPE WITH STRESS

There are not many generalizations one can make with perfect safety about the whole of mankind except for purely anatomical or physiological ones; but it is quite safe to say that every human being alive today is subject to some form of stress or another. If you had never read anything of Freud's work and we had not examined together his ideas on infantile development in Chapter Three, you might perhaps suppose well-cared for babies during their first year of life, to be an exception to this rule, especially if you have only been acquainted with peaceful, placid infants who sleep, feed and smile as required, and never seem to cry, let alone bawl, scream and whimper.

Such contented babies are not, however, an exception. Even if you are not an adherent to Freud's theories it is easy to see that the stresses that small babies encounter must be very numerous. When they are hungry, cold, wet, dirty or lonely they have no means of communicating their specific needs and can only cry (or wait patiently) until somebody notices their plight. If you do follow the Freudian school of thought, then you must add to purely physical stresses the early conflicts we have already discussed in detail; turmoils sufficiently severe to predispose babies towards depressive illness (among other neurotic conditions) later in life, and to lay the foundations of an all-or-nothing personality.

Few people would question the statement that all children and adults have to contend with stress. Children the world over are subject to the ups-and-downs of personal relationships. Affection is to be won from parents; and siblings and peers played with, loved and fought. The hazards of the school community, with the extra burden of homework, school exams and discipline, play a large part in a child's life in developed countries. Elsewhere, where children are not as yet regularly educated, life is on the whole a great deal more stressful, with poverty, disease and hard physical labour sapping their useful energy. One needs also to point out, if only for the sake of completeness, that no adult — be they a wealthy monarch, a scientist of genius, an adored pop star or the Reverend Mother of a community of nuns — is free from the stresses that abound both for everyone living and for the individual at a personal level.

We all know what stress is, although you may pause to think for a moment before defining it. It is of course a stimulant in the external environment which gives rise to the 'flight or fight' mechanism described in the last chapter. But while we are aware of a sudden fright — such as a near-miss car accident — we are not always so aware of the continuous stresses to which we are subject. The stress, for example, of queueing in the rain for a bus when you are late for work or working all day in a small, overheated and claustrophobic office with a set of people, or even one person, with whom you have nothing in common. Most of our routine daily actions are sources of stress. Familiar examples are frequent travel; the constant demand of children, spouse and housework; and either looking for a job, coping with redundancy, or doing your best against competition to retain the job you have. On the economic front, there is worry about your stocks, shares and the stock exchange at one end of the spectrum, or wondering how on earth to make ends meet, at the other.

I have just used the word 'worry'. While it is true that every human being is stressed it is also true to say that not everybody worries. When you think of the stresses in life, it is extremely surprising that this is so, yet it is a fact that very well balanced, philosophical, phlegmatic types of people are often almost, or even entirely, devoid of that reaction. Worry is the response within your mind to a situation, circumstance, or set of facts about which you are concerned. Generally speaking, when worry is felt, the outcome is anticipated but is as yet undetermined. We worry that we may fail an examination or driving test; we worry that we will run out of money before the end of the month; we worry that a breast lump is cancerous; alternatively, we worry that our son or daughter will forget to look left and right before crossing the road on the way to school, or that the roads will be too bad for us to reach an airport in time for an important flight departure.

All worry has one sole determining characteristic: there is always *something* known to us as its cause. When people worry a lot they are sometimes said to worry about nothing. This is not the case for, while they may worry about trivia — and the majority of us worry too much — they cannot worry about *nothing* because by definition this is impossible. If we feel profoundly worried, and yet know no good reason for the foundations of our feelings then we are experiencing not worry but anxiety. As we saw earlier, anxiety symptoms are commonly found part and parcel with depressive illness. Anxiety neurosis, is, in fact, an illness in its own right and results from a strong predisposition to anxiety that has grown so manifest in a personality that it has become one of its chief features.

Anxiety neurosis is a pitiful state and, although different from depression, is capable of being equally incapacitating. This book is aimed at telling you how to cure depression; it does not purport to discuss anxiety neurosis in great detail, nor to explain how to cure that illness. Nevertheless, many depressed people have a pronounced tendency to anxiety, and stress, worry and anxiety — singly or in combination — constitute a strong predisposing factor towards the development of depression. So we will look at each in turn from the point of view of overcoming its effects after taking a quick look at why some people suffer from anxiety in the first place.

Anxiety arises due to turmoil and conflict during the third, or genital, phase of a child's psychological development. This is the time when 'true' sexual feelings first appear and this generally occurs around the age of five to six years, the genital period as a whole lasting until around the age of eight. The conflict associated with this phase of development stems from the association in the child's mind between sexual feelings and guilt, and comes about if the child is mishandled at this particular time. A little boy smacked and scolded for playing with his penis, for example, or a small girl punished for investigating either her own body with her fingers or her brother's external organ from a sense of curiosity, will soon associate sexual exploration with guilt and disgrace.

If the process continues, developing sexuality is transformed into guilt, and the massive psychological damage that results from this transformation manifests itself in one of two ways. One is the development of hysterical tendencies and a hysterical personality, which are not relevant to discussion in this book; and the other is the formation of an anxiety state. Anxiety states are capable of producing genuine organic illness, overwhelming feelings of fear, phobias and sexual impotence.

We have neither the time nor the space to deal with each of these in detail; but it is well worthwhile finding out how early sexuality is mischannelled to produce an anxious personality and the symptoms of an anxiety attack. It is easier to obtain a clearer picture of the mechanism if we first take a quick look at what actually happens during an anxiety attack. Such an attack is a specific phenomenon and not simply another name for feeling very anxious. Another name for it is a 'panic attack' and it consists of the sudden onset of feelings of tremendous fear, accompanied by all the signs of adrenaline and noradrenaline release that we have come to expect at such a time. The person's breathing suddenly becomes rapid and shallow, and he may feel that he is fighting for breath; his eyes, wide open, stare fixedly in front of him; he may be transfixed to the spot, his mouth goes dry, his heart pumps rapidly and the very intensity of the physical symptoms — especially when they occur for the first time — can increase his innate fear to the point at which he believes that he is either about to die or to have a fit.

The affected person is aware of nothing that can cause such a reaction, and it is this that constitutes the hallmark of anxiety attacks and anxiety generally, indicating their marked difference from worry. If you worry, you are only too well aware of what is troubling you; if you are anxious, you have no idea of the cause of your problem. This is because the cause of the anxiety is hidden from consciousness and buried deep in the subconscious mind. Worry, on the other hand, is a conscious activity and nobody who experiences it has any trouble in relating cause and effect.

Because anxiety and anxiety attacks are generated by subconscious conflict, no appropriate conscious action can be taken to allay them. This mental state which Freud referred to as 'free floating anxiety', having once produced an attack is likely to produce similar ones, and a chronic anxiety state generally develops. This means that the person is more or less permanently in a state of nervous anticipation, and mentally and physically geared to the 'flight or fight' reaction. This energy build-up can never be released in a normal way, as there is no appropriate action of which he is consciously aware. There is a profound feeling of anxiety, fear and dread which can vary in intensity from day to day but is constantly present, either occupying the mind in the fullest sense or lying dormant in the background waiting to take over the conscious faculties. He feels as though the sword of Damocles is hanging permanently above his head but does not know when the impending disaster will strike. Ultimately, the tensions within build up to the point at which they erupt into yet another anxiety attack.

Taking an objective look at the mechanisms of such an attack, in which physical manifestations result when internal tension mounts in momentum to discharge point, it is easy to see the parallel between this situation and that of the normal sexual act. In the latter, certainly bodily sensations affect the mind, and the mind works upon body, and great inner tension builds up — but both this and the discharge of energy in orgasm are experienced as exciting and pleasurable anticipation, and equally pleasant release when the climax is reached. The experience, on the other hand, of an anxiety attack both in the moments leading up to it and in the discharge of its physical features, is distinctly unpleasurable; but there is no doubt that it is an abnormal outlet for repressed sexual feeling.

Because of this close relationship between normal sexuality and the anxiety state it is possible to define the relationship with either of these to the other great biological instinct of self-preservation. The physical symptoms of the panic attack — the racing heartbeat, shallow breathing, dilated pupils and bodily muscles primed for immediate action — are the same as those produced by a shock or sudden physical challenge in which flight or fight are necessary. The close similarity between the two leads us to believe that the transformation of the psychic energy into the features of anxiety, rather than that of normal sexual activity, takes place at the most primitive level of instinctive function. So it is worth making a brief mention here of how the mind of a person suffering from anxiety actually copes.

The anxiety, being groundless to the conscious and rational mind, cannot be eliminated, as worry can, by the act of reasoning or by taking active steps to deal with the problem. However, the absorption of the ego by 'free floating' anxiety is an intolerable state of affairs and what are called 'symptom formations' occur. This is simply an unconscious attempt to produce something for the conscious mind to focus upon and to which to attach its anxiety. The symptoms that are formed are only symbols for the underlying, groundless anxiety and affect any particular individual in one of three ways. It may be that purely *physical symptoms* are produced which can ultimately lead to real pathological change in part of the body; frequent gastrointestinal upsets, for instance, may lead eventually to a peptic ulcer or some form of bowel inflammation

Alternatively a *phobia* may develop, another unconscious attempt at substituting the known for the unknown. This reaction is typical of the intellectual type of person and its immediate advantage is that some kind of avoiding action can be taken, at least initially. For example, if the anxiety is dealt with by projecting it on to spiders, cats or black beetles the individual experiencing the phobia will at least be able to provide himself with an explanation for the anxiety he feels and eliminate much of his anxiety simply by avoiding the object of his phobia. The problem with this solution is that the phobia tends to extend outwards from a particular object to include others like it, of the same colour, or the same species or type.

Lastly, internal anxiety can be *projected outwards* and attached to the real problems and worries which other people experience. A person in whom this mechanism would work would be deeply affected by other people's problems and typically take others' troubles upon their own shoulders. .

It should be clear from the above description of anxiety that the depressed person who suffers also from anxiety neurosis is very unfortunate indeed. If his depression is of the reactive type then he will have suffered some recent tragedy or will be caught up in a deeply unpleasant life situation precipitating a depressive reaction, and this will be coupled with a dread of the unknown (free floating anxiety). This in turn will either erupt every now and again in panic attacks or will manifest itself in one of the three other ways I have mentioned.

If the individual concerned suffers from endogenous depression, then his free floating anxiety and its attendant discomfort will accompany the depression reaction which also, to his conscious mind, has no apparent cause. It is little wonder that people in either category (but especially in the latter) sometimes fear that they are going insane.

Let us take a look therefore at what can be done to eliminate the factors of stress, worry and anxiety from our lives as far as possible.

Stress

Not all stress is harmful, and a certain amount of it is essential to us. The right kind of stress provides us with challenge and excitement, quickens the pulse, brightens the eye and keeps us physically and mentally on our toes. An extreme example, of course, is the pursuit of a dangerous sport such as hang gliding, mountaineering or potholing. The constant danger of crashing, slipping or becoming trapped is a very strong stress factor, and the mental alertness and physical agility which result physiologically from this stress, are essential to those who practice such sports, for they need to be on top form at all times.

Other examples of harmless stress factors are choosing to see a thriller or horror film; regular aerobic exercise that taxes the body and stimulates the mind; and attending interviews. In the latter instance although you may feel, as you sit in the waiting room, that your mouth is so dry and your heart is beating so fast that you will not be able to utter a single coherent sentence, nevertheless what normally happens is the reverse. When you come face to face with the prospective employer or the members of the selection committee, the prior stimulation of your 'flight or fight' mechanism usually enables you to give your best performance.

All these harmless stresses, however, have one factor in common: they are all transitory and (even including the interview situation!) they are all undergone voluntarily. Harmful stresses, on the other hand, batter us mercilessly on all sides day after day, week after week. It is no wonder that, in the end, they take their toll.

You will find that unhealthy stresses fall into two categories: those you can do something about and those you will have to learn to react to in such a way that they are incapable of harming you. Stresses about which something can be done are legion and differ from one individual to another. Your main source of stress may be an unhappy marriage, interfering in-laws, self consciousness resulting from a personal weight or beauty problem, an unspoken fear of driving in rush hour traffic, or dislike of your job. Just remember that you have more power than you think over yourself, and the way your life is lived; and just as power begets power, so self-confidence begets further self-confidence. List the stress factors that you know have a solution somewhere, and write down these possible solutions.

If your marriage is unhappy, discuss the subject with your spouse and go to see a marriage guidance counsellor — alone, if necessary; or if your marriage has irretrievably broken down and you would be happier living your own life, summon up your courage and separate.

You have interfering in-laws? Have you ever politely, but effectively, given them a piece of your mind, or have you always put up with them, fearing to offend them? Again, take courage, speak to your husband or wife and, preferably with his or her backing (or if necessary without it), go and indulge in some plain speaking. I do not mean 'have a first-class row'; in fact, if you remain calm, then no row will develop, but make certain that anybody who is a constant interference in your life, be it in-law, parent, relation or friend, is put kindly, but very firmly, in his or her proper place.

If rush hour driving is your problem, refuse to put up with this stress any longer. Either adopt another form of transport, and in cities large enough to have a rush hour there is always a choice, or — better still — ask a patient friend or relation to come out with you in heavy traffic at weekends, when you are not under stresses of other kinds. Even have a few extra driving lessons, if you prefer. Explain your problem to the driving school and instructor and ask for a short course of 'topping up' lessons to increase your self-confidence.

If you have a cosmetic problem or you are very overweight, do something concrete about it. It doesn't matter if your plans to do so in the past have failed, there is no reason why they should this time. Go to see your doctor if you think he is able to give you the advice you need to get started, and either make some enquiries about cosmetic surgery if you have an appropriate physical defect or ask for a diet sheet and arrange to go back regularly, say every two weeks, to be weighed and to report on progress. Alternatively, join Weight Watchers or find a friend who also wishes to slim, and do it in conjunction with him or her.

Finally, if you don't like your job, there are two possible alternatives open to you. If it is the only job of its type available in your area, and will lead shortly and surely to promotion, or if it offers you essential early experience for climbing higher up your chosen tree, then be philosophical about it and count it as one of the stresses which must be temporarily borne and to which you will learn to react as I suggest in the next section. If the job is none of these things, but so far you have been too scared or too lazy to resign, now is the time to act. The money may be essential, so find something else fast and give your notice in. If the money is not essential, merely very pleasant to have and you can do without it for a bit, this is another reason for leaving. The idea is to eliminate every major precipitating cause of depression from your life whenever it is possible to do so. No form of employment can possibly be worth suffering depressive illness for.

How about the stresses that, for the time being at any rate, you will have to bear? It *isn't* possible to stop young children crying, pestering you or catching measles, singly or in unison; and there will still be the crowded supermarkets, the strap-hanging rush hour travel, the accumulating office work or housework, as well as nosey neighbours, awkward colleagues, and your teenage offspring's pop music, friends and untidiness.

You can remove the irritant factor from all the harmful stresses in your daily life and prevent them from causing you any further concern. The secret is to learn the art of relaxation, and before you dismiss this statement as too simplistic and too trite, bear in mind two things. First, that apart from contributing to depressive illness, excessive stress has been directly related by medical research to an increasing number of diseases and conditions. A brief list of these would include: frequent headaches; migraine attacks; digestive upsets; peptic ulcers; diverticular disease; diabetes; infertility; sexual problems; a number of mental disorders; asthma; eczema; psoriasis and many other skin disorders. Stress is also believed to play a major part in the generation of cancer in the body; and is known to be one of the chief precipitating factors with respect to cardiovascular disease, including furred up arteries, high blood-pressure, coronary thrombosis and strokes.

The second thing to remember is that anybody can learn largely to eliminate stress from their lives by relaxation, if they are capable of reading or obeying simple instructions and practising them daily. So first you have to learn how to relax, then you have to learn how to apply this art at a moment's notice when faced with or involved in a stressful situation.

You should begin by finding half an hour every day when you can practise relaxation and adding this important half-hour to the regimen already outlined in the last chapter. Don't say that it is impossible because if you really wish to find half an hour to yourself then you can do so. Choose, for example, thirty minutes after supper when the children are in bed and your husband has settled down with his pipe, slippers and papers; or, if that is equally impossible, try getting up half an hour earlier. Better still, do it last thing at night, half an hour before you get into bed. Go into a room by yourself, and either sit in an armchair or lie on the floor with a cushion under your head. Make sure that you are comfortable but don't actually lie on the bed or sofa because you will probably go to sleep! Lie on your back with both legs out in front of you and your arms by your side. Clench your toes and your foot muscles as firmly as you can without making them go into cramp; and then very slowly *release* the muscles, at the same time closing your eyes and saying the word R-E-L-A-X . . .

Keep your eyes closed gently for the rest of the half-hour. When you have clenched and relaxed your feet and toe muscles, actually *feel* the loose floppy state of relaxation that they are now in. Working up your body — and it is very important to do this systematically — apply this 'clench-relaxation' technique to your ankles, your calf muscles, your thigh muscles, your buttocks, your stomach muscles, your chest and back and shoulder muscles, the muscles of your fingers, hands, forearms and upper arms, your neck muscles and the muscles of your face. You will obviously have to pull ugly faces, frown, grin, etc., in exercising your cheeks, forehead and lips — but don't worry, there is nobody to watch or criticize.

Finally, and this is very important, remember your tongue. Stick it out of your mouth as far and as hard as you can without hurting its root; then slowly withdraw it into your mouth, close your lips and let it just sink back into place, soft and friable, completely passive and relaxed. Your body is now in a state of relaxation, and the degree of relaxation that you achieve will improve with regular practice.

You are now in a position to relax your mind. It is impossible to relax your mind when your body is tense and uncomfortable, and stimulated by light, sound and human voices, so keep the lighting subdued in the room you choose, and close the doors and windows to eliminate extraneous sounds before your start.

First of all, try to think of nothing. You will find the harder you try to think of nothing, the more your mind will persist in thinking of something. I think of nothing (insofar as this is possible) by forming a mental picture of one particular object and holding it in my mind to the exclusion of any other thing. Choose something that you like, that appeals to you and makes you feel calm. I choose to think of a dark red rose, fully open, perfect and wonderfully perfumed. You may have to try hard at first to capture one visual image only in your mind and to hold it there; and that is the reverse of relaxation. So do not try too hard or by what is known as the 'law of reversed efforts' you will fail. If you start by choosing a symbol that appeals to you, and also preferably one which for a number of years has come to mean something special to you within your own personal terms of reference, then you are far more likely to succeed in visualizing it. Just let the mental picture of it drift into your mind and hold it there, and continue to contemplate it as you lie there relaxing for as long as you care to.

I did not devise this system of relaxation. You may already be familiar with it and, if you are not, you will find similar descriptions of how to attain it in library books, magazine articles, textbooks on hypnotherapy, and on cassette tapes which purport to relax you in a similar manner. I do not recommend using the latter for other purposes. To qualify this statement, I should say that a *simple relaxation tape,* taking you step by step through the stages that I have described and aiming only at inducing physical and thus mental relaxation, is harmless and may well be a useful aid. But hypnotherapy cassette tapes which purport to help you to achieve a particular goal, whether this is becoming more self-confident, ceasing to blush or achieving better relationships are, to my mind, suspect. Very susceptible and sensitive individuals may well respond so strongly to these taped suggestions that they reach a crisis point, psychologically speaking, and require the support, the reassurance and the help of an experienced therapist who is not, of course, around to fulfill the role. Generally speaking, I would advise relying upon your own ability to induce relaxation as a means of coping with stress.

Follow the routine I have suggested every day of your life for half an hour, and stress will soon cease to bother you. This is because the repeated daily sessions of thirty minutes of relaxation will enhance your life positively, and help to restore harmony, stability and balance. In the early stages, you will find that you will still require help when faced with the psychological stresses and strains of your daily life. What you do is 'step back' psychologically speaking from the situation which is plaguing you, to recall the sensations of relaxation with which you are becoming familiar. Take a physical step backwards if this is symbolically helpful, let your eyelids droop and your body go slack, sit down if you have the chance, and if not stand but slouch comfortably and relieve tension where any is obvious.

Breathe deeply and slowly, saying the word 'relax' in your mind as you breathe out and after three breaths picture your relaxation image. Once you have practised your relaxation technique often enough you will find that merely summoning up the mental image you associate with your relaxation sessions will induce the same peace and mental harmony, and provide the same impermeability to the slings and arrows of stressful stimuli, that your thirty minutes daily practice period gives you.

You will still reap the benefit of the positive, exciting stresses in your life and dancing, riding and swimming will always thrill you as they have in the past. Classical music, mountaineering or chess will offer the same delights; but the harmful, destructive stresses will lose their ability to disrupt your new-found sense of balance.

Worries

Worries can be treated in a similar manner to stresses. There are worries that you do not have to tolerate; and there are worries about which nothing can be done for the time being. If you have a number of worries that seriously affect the way you feel about life and prompt sporadic attacks of depressive illness, write down a list of them and include every one that you can think of, from the biggest and most pressing to the smallest and most banal. Then consider each in turn and put an asterisk against those which you can eliminate by some action or another. To give you an example, let us suppose that you have the following list of worrying problems:

- You've recently found a small lump in your breast and are worrying about it, but can't pluck up courage to go to the doctor.
- You are worried that your small child, who has just started to walk to school and to return home alone, may forget the kerb drill or be led into danger by a stranger.
- You are worried by the thought of a forthcoming visit to the dentist.

- You are worried because you are twenty years older than your husband or wife, and wonder what it will be like when he or she is fifty and you are seventy.
- You are worried about the possible size of your imminent telephone bill and whether you will be able to meet it.
- You are worried that you often get depressed and feel that the point may come when you are no longer able to cope.

Looking at each of these worries in turn, you can cross the first off straight away. You know in your heart of hearts that you will have to visit the doctor about your lump. Go to the telephone and make the appointment straight away, or ask your husband or best friend to do so on your behalf. Many worries are dispersed by knowledge and if you have only just found a breast lump it cannot be very big. The majority of cancers, (say the word 'cancer' to yourself) can be cured if caught in the early stages (now say the word 'cure'). In any case, the chances are high that your breast lump is mastitis or a benign nodule. Go to your doctor and you achieve two things. Treatment for your lump — and peace of mind.

Regarding the second problem: all children present a certain amount of worry to all caring parents. You cannot be with your son every moment of the day. You may see him safely to the school gates, and five minutes later he may fall down the cloakroom steps and fracture his skull or slip over a greasy spot in the playground and break his leg. Make quite certain that before you let him out on the street, you have explained to him clearly the dangers both of traffic and of friendly strangers. Secondly, make sure that he understands and can repeat your instructions in his own words. Then let him go. You will be doing him a favour, because you will be teaching him to stand on his own feet at an early age, and to acquire a small measure of independence.

The dentist is worrying you. If you don't like your dentist, or if he or she is rough or makes you feel scared — change to a new one, even if this means having to travel a little further. Ask the receptionist at the new dental surgery if you can have a word with the practitioner, and explain that you would like to change because you are particularly nervous. Most dentists, like doctors, appreciate being taken into the confidence of a prospective patient; and you are more than likely to get a sympathetic listener and a considerate dental surgeon. If your worry/fear of dentists amounts to a phobia then this is an aspect of anxiety neurosis and should be treated by a form of psychotherapy, preferably hypnotherapy.

If you are worried about your age in relation to that of your husband or wife — talk about it! You obviously love one another or you wouldn't be worried, so show your love and confidence in your partner by relying on his or her help and willingness to give you reassurance. You cannot alter the age difference and you have probably lived with it for some time. Whenever you find it worrying you or keeping you awake at night, induce a state of physical and mental relaxation and picture your relaxation image. In time it will cease to bother you.

If financial worries keep you awake at night, you have my sympathy. The majority of people, other than millionaires, perhaps, worry about money. Certainly some people worry because they have too much of it, and don't know what to do with it; but the majority of us worry about how to make ends meet. Be careful and avoid extravagance while allowing yourself some fun; and if you are not well organized, take a book about housekeeping out of the library and read the chapter on home economics. Do the best that you can and if you feel that some state benefit is owing to you which you are not receiving — pay a visit to your Citizens Advice Bureau.

Finally, you are concerned about the fact that you are worried and get depressed, and fear that the day may come when you can cope no longer. You can at least cease to worry about that. Having got so far with this book you have read and absorbed many tips, tried and tested over the years, on how to go about coping with any aspect of your problems. If you follow faithfully the plan that I devised, tailoring it here and there to suit your own personal needs, you will cope with any eventuality.

Here is a trick I personally employ for coping with persistent worries that continue to nag despite my efforts to be rid of them. Stand opposite an open window and look up at the sky; make sure that you have not got anyone in your immediate vicinity who may distract your attention. Look upwards into the clouds (not directly into the sun) and project against them a picture from your visual imagination of whatever is worrying you, be it a dentist standing at the ready with a drill, your small son being offered sweets by the driver of a passing car, or the bailiffs knocking at the door because you cannot pay your telephone bill. Look upwards at the empty expanse until you can actually see in your mind a clear representation of the worrying factor, then, with an imaginary fibre tipped pen, draw a thick flamboyant coloured circle all the way round your mental picture, just as a cartoonist might do. This is successfully circumscribing whatever factors are worrying you and preventing them from getting to you. Then jerk your head slightly and feel your own power sending your cartoonist's balloon upwards with its thick, colourful perimeter enclosing the factors that previously had such power to worry and torment you. Let this balloon caricature sail upwards getting smaller and smaller and then, when you will it, let it just break and disperse, flinging tiny, harmless fragments of itself in all directions. Imagine them, in your mind's eye, dispersing here and there over the surface of the earth at the total mercy of the four winds, broken down into the tiniest elemental constituents.

Come back slowly to your present surroundings and your worry will be with you no longer. Should it dare to repeat its trick of trying to torment you, form another balloon in the sky and get rid of it again. *You* are the one with unlimited power. Use it and nothing can harm you.

Anxiety

We have seen that anxiety is a neurotic manifestation of repressed sexual energy. Mild anxiety can be coped with by regular relaxation sessions. If you benefit from the regimen up to a particular point and yet can get no further because you continue to be plagued by free floating anxiety which makes you feel physically and psychologically uncomfortable and depressed at the same time — with, perhaps, occasional anxiety attacks — then have a word with your doctor. Ask whether he or she can refer you either to a psychodynamic psychotherapist or a hypnotherapist (see Chapter Seven). My own preference lies with the hypnotherapist, simply because I have practised this art myself and am more acquainted with this form of therapy, but any well qualified and experienced psychotherapist should be able to help you. If you can afford to go privately, do so, provided you are prepared to enter into a frank and co-operative relationship with your therapist so that he or she can help you to the fullest extent.

I would recommend private treatment if you can possibly manage this as it does ensure regular sessions of reasonable length for as long as you require them. Tell your therapist on your first visit, or in an introductory letter or telephone call, about your depressive illness and about this book and the regimen suggested. Obtain his or her approval in the first place and then both of you will know where you stand and there will be no question of divided loyalties at a later date should your therapist, unaware that you are following a basic life reorganizing programme, suggest a similar routine to you. In the next chapter we are going to look at the third stage of your personal programme which will help you to relearn the art of thinking.

9.

YOUR PERSONAL PROGRAMME: POSITIVE THOUGHT

Asking you to relearn the art of thinking sounds a very tall order. Although the brain of each one of us is potentially capable of an infinite number of thoughts, of absorbing thousands of viewpoints and weighing up, analysing and drawing conclusions from billions of different sets of circumstances, we none of us use our brains to full capacity. It has been estimated in fact that the average man or woman uses no more than ten per cent of his or her total mental faculties; even a learned professor may not use a higher proportion of his total brain capacity than the rest of us. A highly talented actor, on the other hand, writer, musician or poet may well utilize between fifteen and twenty per cent of a "total thought capacity" because in addition to his powers of reasoning he makes active use of a powerful imagination.

Even this leaves a good eighty per cent of mental 'human potential' untapped and unused and puts one in mind of the mental iceberg discussed in Chapter Three, where the conscious mind represents the visible tip and the subconscious the hidden bulk. I am not suggesting that we use only our conscious minds and neglect the subconscious. We can make best use of our mental faculties by the combined usage of conscious with subconscious — of thought, perception, cognitive powers, combined with memory, imagination and the recognition of instinctive urges.

Why is the way we think so important in our plan to cure ourselves of depressive illness? As I have mentioned earlier the thoughts of a depressive person run along familiar lines of doom, self-blame and despair. Indeed, in the severest form of depression, when the patient is in what I personally call an intellectual stupor, I maintain that little 'thought' takes place at all. There is a constant agonizing awareness of intense misery, just as there is when you have had an accident, or are in severe pain resulting from an illness, and your mental faculties are completely absorbed in trying to cope with the pain. Similarly in severe depression, your mental faculties cease their normal range of everyday processes and, so far as they function at all, are absorbed into that state of mental torpor. Just like stresses, established thought patterns are not that easy to get rid of. Try too hard not to think about something and by the same law of reversed effort I referred to earlier, you will be quite sure of thinking of that very thing to the exclusion of all others.

What I am going to write now is perhaps the most essential part of the entire book. It is the nucleus of the information that I want to give to you and is in essence a mode of thinking that, if you wish, you can assume, establishing yourself from that time onwards as master or mistress of your own emotional and mental life and impregnable to further attacks of depression and anxiety.

One of your first objections to this idea, even before you know the details, may well be that *you* cannot do anything to shift the heavy cloak of depressive illness that suddenly descends and envelops you like a black shroud. Because, as I have pointed out several times in this book you, or the 'self' part of you, is depleted of energy and initiative, and thereby too weak and feeble to protest at the enshrouding.

Of course this is true! What I am advising is that you spend your present or next remission from depressive illness equipping yourself with the right mental weapons to defeat the enemy of depressive thought patterns next time they threaten to arise. The most important piece of information that I can give you is that you do not have to be the passive victim of depression, with or without attendant anxiety, in the same way that a young child in the first few years at school is the passive recipient of childhood infectious illnesses, and may or may not contract them, depending upon previous contacts with the illness concerned and the presence or absence of protective antibodies. When and whether you next get depressed is *not* the luck of the draw. It is not *inevitable* that you will continue to suffer from depressive episodes. You are not 'fated', 'tainted', 'touched with the mark of Cain', or otherwise marked out from the rest of the human race by the Fates who have decreed that, as part of your worldly lot, you are to suffer the misery of neurotic depression for the whole of your adult life.

You may feel as though you can do nothing about it. This is a falsehood and is in part due to an underlying lack of self esteem and insufficient self-confidence. I do not want to quote the Bible at you but there is far more truth in the statement that 'Faith can move mountains' than the vast majority of people would ever credit. I cannot tell you how faith-healing works, I cannot explain how the placebo effect of a drug or physical manoeuvre can affect a patient so intensely that his symptoms stop forthwith. I cannot explain how the sheer determination to achieve a goal, to survive in the face of clearly impossible odds or to recover from a seemingly fatal illness succeeds. I only know that the achievers in this world do not necessarily possess physical, spiritual and mental powers that you and I lack. The way in which they are exceptional is in their recognition and application of the powers they own; and, correspondingly, the way in which the rest of us are mostly unexceptional is that we accept, unquestioningly, the role of passive victim.

There is, of course, a certain element of stupidity in the latter attitude but there is a much larger element of mental laziness. To conquer an affliction, to achieve a goal, to overcome a handicap (and a tendency to depressive illness *is* a handicap) requires thought, determination, effort and self-discipline. Many of us would prefer to put up with what we have, rather than reorganize ourselves and our lives into a better shape. My reason for writing this book is to tell anyone who suffers from depression, or anyone who is concerned about a friend or relative who does so, that the end of the illness is in sight if you are prepared to make sufficient effort to see that it is so.

Early thought patterns arise in ways we have described earlier in the book and are determined to a certain extent by early instinctual conflicts. These thought patterns flourish and establish themselves as a result of our experience of relationships and the outside world. If, for example, when we are young we develop a tendency to the all-or-nothing reaction or turn our rage inwards because we are shown insufficient love and concern, then the way in which we approach our environment and other people will be coloured by the effect these tendencies had on our young minds. We are not *bound* to react in a particular way because of a set of experiences but we are very likely to do so and, once the all-or-nothing reaction manifests itself a few times in a young and developing child, we have a tendency to be blissfully happy or profoundly unhappy and this way of thinking becomes habitual. We expect, barely before we wake up in the morning, to be either ecstatic or in the doldrums, and so the situation is a self perpetuating one and we are invariably one or the other.

Likewise, if our 'down' periods are characterized from a very early age by feelings of self-blame, self-castigation and a strong sense of inadequacy then we cannot be surprised if this tendency becomes an automatic reaction, if we do not take steps to see that it is otherwise.

Start your attempts to combat your negative thinking patterns when you are not depressed, have time to do so, and are feeling reasonably optimistic. There is no point in attempting to do this when you are afflicted by profound feelings of guilt, unworthiness, inferiority, wickedness and inevitable damnation; then you cannot be expected to see the wood for the trees. Start by taking your notebook, possibly the same one in which you have made a list of your stresses as explained in the previous chapter, and write down three thoughts that regularly recur to you when you are depressed. I have mentioned earlier the presence, in most people suffering from depressive illness, of a prodromal phase through which they pass from an episode of normality into one of moderate or severe depression. Very often a change in thought pattern is a major feature of the prodromal period and you may well find that certain signs and symptoms appear in a regular pattern before an episode of depression becomes established.

Perhaps you wake up feeling less confident than usual, maybe you react even more sensitively than usual to criticism or unkind remarks. Perhaps you find yourself brooding over past events that generally do not bother you; maybe, too, you often find that preoccupation with the past is inextricably bound with feelings of self blame and guilt. You should in such and such a situation have done so and so, and if you had then a particular, regrettable event would not have occurred.

Alternatively, you should not, you now realize, have reacted in such and such a way, or said such and such a thing, but you did. Please believe that everyone on earth, from the Archbishop of Canterbury to the Yorkshire Ripper, from Her Majesty the Queen to the most desolate victim of homelessness sleeping on the embankment, has *something* in his or her past with which to reproach himself. This applies to everybody you know, everybody you feel is superior to you and everybody in front of whom you feel you have made a fool of yourself. You are no exception to the rule, no worse than anybody else and in many cases, although you cannot see it, you may well be vastly superior. When you choose your three thoughts to write down then make sure that you choose three that usually present themselves to your conscious mind in the earliest phase of an attack.

Now have a short break, make yourself a cup of coffee, sit down and a few minutes later have another look at the three thought patterns. Doesn't all this intense guilt seem a little unnecessary and a little wearing when you look at it in the cold light of day? Look around you in your present normal and non-depressed state — is the world such a terrible place? If your own environment is ugly, use your present remission to redecorate it, rearrange it or at least give it a thorough spring-clean. The transformation that can be effected by stripping old paint and varnish off battered furniture and painting drab walls white or buttercup yellow is quite astonishing.

Relationships have already been discussed under the heading of stresses and any that bother you must be dealt with accordingly. What else do you think about? You secretly dread a nuclear holocaust and feel that the world about you has no real substance and that you and everything you know is going to be enveloped sooner rather than later in unimaginable horror. Well it's not going to happen today; it probably won't happen tomorrow and the chances are reasonable that it isn't going to happen next week. I am not being flippant or facetious about matters of world or cosmic importance, nor about the future or the lack of it for mankind. I am talking to you, as a person who has suffered in the past from depressive illness and, since you alone cannot alter the tide of events and may not be in a position to devote your life to joining with others to try to change it, you may as well live as happily as you can. This is not shrugging off responsibility, it is, in fact, accepting responsibility for yourself and your own limitations and liberating yourself from fear to cope with the responsibilities immediately surrounding you.

Symptoms

You now have three major thought changes that are no more nor less than symptoms, or warning signs, of possible sickness. If a person suffers from migraine attacks but is provided with a bottle of tablets which will abort an attack providing that he takes one at the first sign that an attack is imminent he would acknowledge a tendency to migraines but may say that he cannot claim to have had an actual attack for years. Likewise this deflation of mood, fear, anxiety and misery that you start to feel when depressive illness is threatening, can be regarded in the same light as other clinical conditions. Just because the symptoms in your own illness are a descent in mood and a feeling of self blame, there is no reason to allow these to affect or alter your personality, any more than a throbbing pain in the temple should affect the migraine sufferer's personality when an attack is near. There is no truth in or foundation for your feelings of profound unworthiness and the essential secret of coping with the early stage of depression is to recognize it for what it truly is, the symptom of an illness, no more and no less.

Once you have accepted this fact about symptoms and signs you will rob negative thoughts of their ability to harm you. You can achieve this objectivity by retraining your thought patterns along two positive lines. Firstly, by adopting the habit of relegating all negative thoughts to the category of symptoms of a nuisance illness which lacks the power to do you any real harm, and, secondly, by following through the various stages of your personal programme. There are also two techniques which you can learn which will help you a great deal. They are affirmations and autohypnosis.

Affirmations. Many people are familiar with the Coué technique developed earlier this century for improving self-confidence. Émile Coué suggested that people lacking confidence should repeat to themselves, several times each day the following phrase: 'Every day, in every way I'm getting better and better'. It sounds a small thing and you may think that there is no point in your reciting it because it obviously isn't true and you don't believe it. But this way of thinking is muddling and destructive. You don't have to deserve the expression before you are entitled to recite it. Your recitation of it under your breath several times a day is a positive action, and improved self-confidence will be the effect or outcome.

How does this work? It works by the installation of a way of thinking into your subconscious mind by constant repetition. The phrase, once you've learnt it, becomes so familiar that you can actually think or do something entirely different while repeating it mechanically to yourself. This is the way, of course, in which sleep tapes work — tapes that purport to alter your way of thinking in a positive manner simply by your switching on a tape recorder and playing them over in your bedroom within hearing distance but while you are asleep. Your conscious mind is otherwise engaged in each of these two instances but, far from being out of reach, your subconscious is more accessible than usual and vulnerable to the imprint of a repeated message. Be as distracted as you like while serving up dinner or setting the dials on your washing machine, preoccupation with other affairs will in no way detract from the successful outcome.

The affirmation quoted above works very well for many people, but something rather different may be more applicable to you. You may prefer to say, for instance, 'Every day in every way my happiness is more firmly secured' or, 'Every day that passes I grow more and more self-confident'. It doesn't matter what you choose; choosing an affirmation, though, is a very important part of altering and affecting the way you think. If two or more affirmations appeal to you and you can't choose between them, that's equally fine. Choose one at a time, use that for a spell until you feel that you have extracted every ounce of benefit from it and go on to using the next one and the next.

It also helps to write your affirmation down, not just once when you are composing it but on odd scraps of paper instead of doodling. This also helps to imprint the affirmation in your sub-conscious mind. It is, of course, essential that any affirmation should be positive in nature! This means avoiding words such as 'no' and 'not' and phrasing every intention in positive terms. This applies to all suggestions you make to yourself.

Autohypnosis. You may want to learn autohypnosis either from a hypnotherapist, which is perhaps the best way, or from a good book dealing with the subject. Otherwise you can follow my suggestions and, if you are naturally a good subject and persevere, you may find the details I give perfectly adequate.

The point of autohypnosis in your case is further to rid yourself of negative ways of thinking; to erect a form of protection against stresses, anxieties and other sources of bother and to establish within yourself an inner core of stability and self-confidence making you invulnerable to the effects of old habits.

You will find that hypnotizing yourself into a state of light trance is a very similar feeling to your daily periods of physical and mental relaxation. What you are actually doing is allowing your consciousness or conscious mind to sink down to the meeting point between it and the subconscious. This is a thin barrier or borderline, which you pass twice every twenty-four hours when you are falling asleep or waking up, but, instead of passing into oblivion as you do when you lose consciousness altogether and fall into proper sleep, you remain self-aware in a relaxed and drowsy state. Because your awareness is linking the conscious and subconscious regions of your mind you can relay instructions and suggestions from the former to the latter. When you are about to start your first session of autohypnosis decide beforehand on a scene, such as lake, a river or a sunken garden that you would be happy to sit in, in your imagination, for a few minutes. It can even be somewhere that you know. Now breathe in and out deeply as I suggested and relax every part of yourself; when you get to the point where you would normally picture your rose or rainbow or cloud or the symbol you have chosen as representative of peace and tranquillity, picture instead the scene you have chosen beforehand. See yourself in your imagination standing at the top of a path several feet above the scene which is reachable by means of five shallow steps.

The number of steps is important and you should decide upon the number you are going to see before you start the autohypnosis session. If for instance your favourite scene is a room in a basement flat which you normally see from the top of a flight of eleven or twelve or twenty stairs then choose that scene by all means and give it the appropriate number of steps. If this is not the case, choose a scene with a staircase leading down to it with any definite number of steps between five and ten.

There you are then, completely relaxed, tranquil, with your eyes closed and breathing deeply and slowly; picture your scene and stand at the top of your stairway in your imagination. Walk to the top of the steps and say, as you take the first step downwards, 'deeper', pause and then take the next step and again repeat the word in your mind, slowly and silently, 'deeper'. Pause on each step and say 'deeper' as you take each step downwards until you reach the bottom; you should then be in a relaxed and pleasant state of autohypnotic trance. Emphasis can be given to the word 'deeper' by adding qualifiers such as 'even', 'still', 'yet' and so on.

At this point you are highly receptive to beneficial suggestions that your subconscious mind can accept. Choose a simple suggestion and use the same one, repeated several times over, each time you go into autohypnosis. When you really feel that one has taken effect, choose another from which you feel you may benefit. Say during the first few sessions for instance, 'I am slowly growing more confident'. Repeat this silently in your mind over and over to yourself as you stand or sit peacefully in the scene which you can see vividly in your mind's eye. Enjoy the scenery, the sunshine and the flowers, or whatever the environment is that you have chosen, repeating the suggestion. Then for a short while project yourself from that environment into an imaginary situation where you would normally be uncomfortable and lacking confidence, *but* see yourself as confident and master or mistress of that situation. Now return to your chosen environment and repeat the suggestion a few more times.

When you have finished stay in that safe state for about seven to ten minutes, walk back to the steps and as you climb each step, slowly and deliberately say to yourself as you pause on each one, the word 'lighter'. As you reach the top of your steps you will have returned to your usual state of pleasant relaxation, with your mind in peaceful repose and your body comfortably relaxed. You are then in a position to lie there for a few more moments or minutes and to end the session as and when you choose.

There is nothing to fear in autohypnosis. If you cannot manage it yourself get some help from an experienced hypnotherapist. He will help you to enter a state of trance and give you what is called a post-hypnotic suggestion which will enable you far more easily to go into a light trance when you try by yourself. Do not think that you will get 'stuck' in a state of trance, immobilized and helpless should the phone ring or a sudden emergency arise. Your trance is light and will be immediately broken thus allowing you to do whatever is necessary. Should you prove a very good subject and able to relax easily and induce a light trance, you may find as you practise that the depth of your trance increases and that you go quite deep. This is nothing to fear either and should prove a very pleasant experience. If you go deep enough you will simply fall asleep and wake up naturally.

Make sure that you choose a beneficial and positive suggestion before you start your autohypnosis session. The potential benefit this method has to offer is enormous, but do not be tempted to use this potent technique if you are feeling in a destructive and highly negative mood. Turn to one of the physical methods I have described in Chapter Seven. Go for a jog, busy yourself with a hobby or discuss your problems with a close friend. Wait until you are feeling comfortably positive again and are wishing to cure yourself of recurrent depressive episodes, for that is the time when autohypnosis will prove most beneficial to you.

10.

FACING THE FUTURE

You will see from the advice I gave at the end of the last chapter, that a systematic approach is best for many people in following the three main stages of my personal programme. This ensures that when you (or a depressed person for whom you are caring), start to follow it, you will have recovered temporarily from a severe depressive episode, and be capable of starting off with the suggestions in your Personal Programme: The Physical Approach.

Do not try to achieve everything at once, follow the steps that I suggest in this section and alter the structure of your life successfully. This is a major step forward and should improve your condition to the point at which you can start the next phase of the programme. If you feel in deep personal need of psychotherapy don't hesitate in seeking a therapist at the earliest opportunity. I do advise you though to take some measures to help yourself before turning to him for treatment. Self-help will generate sufficient improvement for you to be able to operate with your therapist to your mutual advantage. If you turn to a therapist, or one is found for you when you are fairly badly depressed, you may well find that you do not profit from the sessions to the same extent as you would if you had waited until your depression was starting to respond to my preliminary suggested approaches. Deal with stress, worry and anxiety as soon as you are comfortably able to and start the relaxation sessions at your earliest opportunity.

There is no definite time scale and it is theoretically possible to tackle the problem from all the angles I have suggested more or less simultaneously. Nevertheless, I have arranged the three stages of the programme in the particular order I have given because the physical methods are the easiest to follow and to put into operation. Get those underway and then turn your attention to dealing with stress, worry and anxiety, and endeavour to master the art of relaxing physically and mentally.

Let us suppose that you have followed the three stages of my plan, are successfully noting the early symptoms of a threatened attack (which should, incidently, become less and less frequent) and are relegating negative thoughts, if they arise, firmly to the realm of 'irritating symptoms'. You must now re-double your efforts in one direction or another; either greater physical activities or more evening relaxation and perhaps extra affirmation. The tool to use is almost bound to be apparent as you will feel a need in a particular direction.

Perhaps you have got so far and wonder if there is any further way in which you can progress further. Yes, of course there is! Health is more than an absence of disease, it is a positive, precious, vital state. No doubt you experience this sensation physically and mentally when you rub yourself down after a cold shower or splash in the morning, or when you have been jogging or perhaps at the end of a vitalizing swim. One of the most important aspects of life is the ability and the opportunity to enjoy it. Having succeeded so far this is how you should go about it. Expand in all the directions you have always longed to take and have never had the nerve to try (until now, that is). Now is your opportunity, since you are refusing to worry, are unruffled by daily stresses and are successfully ridding yourself of anxiety symptoms. Put every aspect of the depressive phase of your life *behind you* and do something you really want to do.

It sounds trite to give the advice 'take up a hobby', it sounds a bit like going to boring evening classes, trying to knit when you can't even bear the sight of knitting needles or bumping uncomfortably about horseback around a riding track in an effort to master the art of riding. Don't take up a hobby without real motivation. Do something that appeals to you — there must be something — have you ever secretly longed to play the violin? Would you adore to go hot air ballooning? Would you love to be able to ice and decorate cakes to a professional standard? Would you rather rear hamsters, take up freelance journalism or throw in your job in the city, together with your season ticket and smart suit? Start your own import/export agency, home decorating business or expensive hand-made chocolate home industry?

One of the objects of the course you have been following has been to teach and help you to use your imagination more often and to great benefit. Sit back in a comfortable chair with a glass of wine or a cup of coffee, put your feet up on your best coffee table (I don't have to tell you to relax!) and ask yourself the question, 'What would I actually like to do?'

Now I'm not suggesting that you effect a major change in your life overnight, particularly one which might disrupt the family economy, but *I am* asking you to give yourself a goal that you are tremendously interested in and enthusiastic about and consequently to plan carefully, methodically and wisely with your partner, if you have one, towards obtaining it. It goes without saying that, for the sake of domestic harmony, this must be a mutually acceptable goal. If it is not and you would still like to achieve your dream quite desperately, you will have to decide whether it remains worth pursuing. Don't disrupt a happy marriage. But if a change of lifestyle in the direction you long to take, would be a major step in relieving you of your tendency to depressive episodes and produce a better, happier you, then you are entitled to go ahead with your plan, providing of course that your partner and the rest of the family do not suffer as a result.

If you don't work at all, perhaps now is the time to take up a hobby as I have suggested, or even a part-time job. I am well aware from years of experience of talking to depressed people that boredom is as conducive to a state of depression as activity is conducive to high spirits. You may have been prevented in the past from working by reason of your illness. On the other hand you may not need the money but, if you do suffer from lack of occupations at home and would like to venture out into a part-time office or shop job, now is the time to give it serious consideration. Buy a paper or visit an employment agency, write some letters and award yourself a star of merit every time you get short listed for interview. Go along anyway for practice, providing of course, you are reasonably interested in the job on offer and refuse to get despondent every time you are turned down. Nowadays this has little or nothing to do with poor standards in the applicants concerned: it is more likely to be simply the luck of the draw where a dozen or a score of people are all competing for the same vacancy. Smile and try again but don't let it be too important to you.

Keep a record book. This is a sensible thing to do, not a childish practice harking back to schooldays. Note down your affirmations, the length of time each one was used and its positive effects. Record *all* the tiny ways in which you are improving. Write down a couple of goals and set yourself a reasonable date by which you will have done something towards achieving them; as soon as you have completed the task write down the result. If your attempt was unsuccessful write down the reason why.

Another angle from which you can approach your overall goal of starting to live life fully and enjoyably, is to look for somebody else worse off than yourself and try giving instead of taking. This is not just a good Christian principle for the saintly few, for it is a fact that one can receive a lot of satisfaction, justifiable self-esteem and a renewed sense of purpose in giving help or pleasure to somebody in need. Volunteer to do a few hours a week in a local hospital or old people's home. Sell flags for the RSPCA or the Blind; contact Age Concern, Save the Children Fund, the NSPCC — any organization that takes your fancy. Why not the Samaritans, once you are well and truly over succumbing to your old depressive episodes and feel that you would like to give of your experience and help others who are afflicted as you once were.

Finally, refuse to be beaten! We *all* have an off-day, a fit of the blues, tragic events in our lives which temporarily overwhelm us, or a viral illness such as influenza, glandular fever or shingles, which predictably leaves its convalescent victims in a state of clinical depression. You *know* that a bad spell in your life, just as it has a beginning, must have an end. And, by the time you have successfully incorporated all three phases of my self-help programme into your life, you will know that there is no reason for you ever to suffer from depression again.

The very best of luck to you!

INDEX